Awakening to the Good

by

Claire Myers Owens

THE BOOK TREE
San Diego, California

ISBN 978-1-58509-132-4

Cover layout by Toni Villalas

Also by Claire Myers Owens

Discovery of the Self
Zen and the Lady (Book Tree edition 2002)

Published by
The Book Tree
P O Box 16476
San Diego, CA 92176
www.thebooktree.com

We provide fascinating and educational products to help awaken the public to new ideas and information that would not be available otherwise.
Call 1 (800) 700-8733 for our *FREE BOOK TREE CATALOG*.

With Love and Gratitude

For Thursty

SMALL ECSTASIES

FOREWORD

The book you now hold is a little-known classic in the literature of human potential. When it was first published in 1958, with the title *Awakening to the Good*, the audience for works about this subject was far smaller than today — the term "human potential" itself was hardly known — and only a few thousand copies were sold before it went out of print.

Nevertheless, the reception it got was most gratifying to the author. Comments flowed in from academic and religious luminaries such as Abraham Maslow, Carl Jung, Aldous Huxley, Albert Schweitzer, Swami Nikhilananda of the Ramakrishna Order, Edmond Sinnott, Raynor Johnson, Henry Margenau, Roberto Assagioli, F.S.C. Northrop, Gordon Allport and Hadley Cantril. Maslow, then chairman of the psychology department at Brandeis University, said, "Exciting, fascinating! I read it at one sitting." Huxley remarked, "It brings out the all important fact that religion is concerned primarily with the immediacy of being." Margenau, professor of physics and philosophy at Yale, said its "insights are deep and remarkable...It inspired me." Gordon Allport, professor of psychology at Harvard, said the author's "luminous experiences are a challenge [to] psychology" and another psychologist, Hadley Cantril, professor at Princeton, said, "I read it with immense interest, most congenial to me."

A quarter of a century later, at a time when world crisis looms larger than ever, conditions are right to reissue a work that speaks to the heart of humanity. Originally described by the publisher as being "in the tradition of Whitman, Emerson and William James," its theme is awakening and transcendence. If ever there was a time to awaken, it is now, and if ever there was a person devoted to awakening — herself and others — it was Claire Myers Owens.

She was born Clairene Myers on February 11, 1896 in Rockdale, Texas to a family of genteel, conservative, fundamentalist Christians, although her father espoused Christian Science. Raised as a gentlewoman, a southern belle, she was soon to rebel against the provincialism of her upbringing. In 1916 she earned a bachelor of science degree in home economics from Texas Woman's University. Later in life she undertook post-graduate work of a different sort at Columbia and Yale. Before her advanced studies occurred, however, she had to break away from her family to seek freedom of thought and action. This she did, though it was most painful for everyone involved. "When I went away to college," she told a reporter late in life, "I realized that there was another big world out there. I rebelled against everything I'd known. I left home because I wanted to be myself." Freedom never comes easily, but it is infinitely worthwhile.

During her early years Claire did settlement house and social work in Chicago, New York City and in an Alabama mining camp. Her wide range of experiences included living in a commune in the Blue Ridge Mountains of Virginia and as a manager and buyer for several well-known New York book shops. An early advocate of women's rights, she published a novel, *The Unpredictable Adventure*, in 1935 which was concerned with the adventures of a young woman named Tellectina (intellect) seeking independence and Certitude in the Forbidden Country of Nithking (thinking). Two brief marriages preceded her third and final marriage to Thurston Owens, who settled her in New Haven, where they had a long and happy relationship. She never had children.

In spite of her satisfying marriage and comfortable existence (her last husband was quite well-to-do), Claire felt a spiritual restlessness that was to become outright misery for her — the suffering of ego-death. *Small Ecstasies/Awakening* is the record of her discovery of trans-egoic states and her exploration of their significance for the human race. Its subtitle in the original edition was "Psychological or Religious?" This denoted Claire's concern for understanding her own and others' experiences of transcendence and for explaining them in a way that resolved the apparent dichotomy between science (of which psychology is a part) and religion. In her spontaneous "awakening to the good" that is inherent in all people, she saw the key to overcoming perennial problems besetting humanity. She had lived through two world wars, and the matter of man's inhumanity to man concerned her to the point of deep, depressing anguish.

Ecstasy, she maintained, is the key to spiritual revelation that alone can cure humanity's sickness. Ecstasy, from *ex stasis*, means, literally speaking, release from a rigid and confining form or condition—movement beyond the status quo. *Ekstasy* is the ancient Greek word for out-of-body experience. But Claire's spontaneous awakenings were not, strictly speaking, parapsychological. They were of a higher order altogether: transpersonal or spiritual. They were psychic in the original sense of the word "psyche," meaning soul. Ekstasy means "the flight of the soul," and Claire's long-sought but nonetheless surprising soul-flights released her momentarily from the bonds of ego and gave her insight into the deeper strata of human consciousness that exist beyond the ego. Amazing grace...

However, the experiences described in this book were not the final revelation or release for Claire. Her hunger for enlightenment was to continue beyond what she tells here. Two other books — *Discovery of the Self* (1963) and *Zen and the Lady* (1979) — and her final, unpublished manuscript, *Meditation and the Lady*, record her journey into light.

Discovery of the Self, presently out of print, may be reissued soon. In his introduction to it, Anthony Sutich, cofounder with Maslow of the Association for Transpersonal Psychology, said it is "a remarkable work about a remarkable woman." It is, if you will, a sequel to *Small Ecstasies/Awakening* because it explores the ways that mystical experience and self-realization can be deliberately induced in people, deepened and made stable, so that the Self beyond self can shine forth in all and become the basis for a humane society of wise and loving people.

Zen and the Lady tells of Claire's training in Zen Buddhism, begun at 74, a year after her husband died in 1969. At an age when most would be content to do nothing, Claire left her mansion, servants and comfortable life to begin "the steep path" to enlightenment. She moved to Rochester, New York (which she calls Snowbound in the book) to study Zen under the spiritual direction of her roshi, Philip Kapleau, at his center there. Her remarkable account of her personal struggles and "larger ecstasies" in this sacred tradition has moved its readers deeply. Though the book sold only modestly, well-known figures in the fields of consciousness research and spiritual studies have responded to it with praise. Ken Wilber, editor-in-chief of *ReVision* and author of *The Spectrum of Consciousness* and *The Atman Project* said, "I found it absolutely fascinating and a totally absorbing story, a superb blend of autobiographical remembrance and sophisticated psychological insight." Dr. Jean Houston, author of *Mind Games* and *The Possible Human*, called it "magnificent" and "a beautiful spiritual story for people of all religions." The *Journal of Transpersonal Psychology* reviewed it as "a treasure trove...of wisdom." Dr. Willis Harman, president of The Institute of Noetic Sciences and a member of the University of California's board of trustees, said, "Thank you for being an inspiration to us all." Professor Kenneth Ring, author of *Life at Death*, declared, "*Zen and the Lady* will become a classic in its genre." Parapsychologist Charles Tart said it was "fascinating."

Claire lived four years beyond the publication of *Zen and the Lady*. They were years of deep fulfillment, despite failing health. "Illness, death and aging don't worry me a bit," she said in a 1979 interview, when she was 83.

So rich did her life seem, in the moment and in retrospect, that she was moved to begin a sequel to her last book. *Meditation and the Lady* reviewed her life from the perspective of meditation's power to heal body, mind and spirit. It was, like all her other works, a love-offering to the world who are the children she never had. The fascinating memoirs contain much new material about her early life, including an account of a date she had with the novelist Thomas Wolfe. However, she did not live to complete the final chapter of *Meditation*. In a sense, that incompleteness is an appropriate symbol of life as an unfinished story whose ending lies only in complete release from the time-bound state of consciousness that is ego. In absolute self-transcendence, there is nothing left to say.

Claire died on the afternoon of May 7, 1983, quietly passing on in her apartment. She had fallen and injured herself several weeks earlier, and had to be hospitalized. She seemed to recuperate, and returned home to be cared for by friends and a nurse who looked after her daily needs while she rested. But the strain upon her health was too great.

Three days after her death, Claire's body was cremated while a close friend from the Zen Center chanted Buddhist sutras. A full Buddhist ceremony, led by Philip Kapleau, was conducted on May 15 and her ashes were returned to the earth in a beautiful garden.

And so passed a great lady. At the funeral, one of her friends, Barbara Percy, offered this summary of Claire's life: "Claire sought to find the balance, to synthesize East and West, the Buddha and the Christ, the right and left hemispheres of reason and intuition, science and religion, that these might be reconciled at the fulcrum in Unity, in Oneness, in Love, being Whole and Healed. She sought to be personally transmuted by the Alchemy of Life, and thus submitted herself to the Crucible, that the dross might be eliminated and the pure gold extracted to shine forth as the Radiant Light in the Mystical Union of self with Self."

To that I say, in recognition of Claire's Christian beginnings, "Amen." And in recognition of her Buddhist orientation at her life's close, it is not, I trust, disrespectful to say that the world is more "buddha-ful" because of Claire. Her memorabilia and manuscripts now reside in the archives of her alma mater, Texas Woman's University, in Denton, Texas. I, as her friend and literary advisor, have become executor of her publications. It is my fervent hope that her literary legacy may serve as she wished — to nurture in people their potential to awaken to the good, the beautiful and the true that are timeless aspects of their own Self.

John W. White
Cheshire, Connecticut
June 1983

CARL JUNG
> "Tell the truth and take the consequences. That's what I have been doing all my life. Expect to be misunderstood. *People fear truth.*"

ARNOLD TOYNBEE:
> "Spiritual struggle seems likely to be the most crucial episode in the next chapter of the history of mankind."

ALDOUS HUXLEY:
> "Systematic reasoning is something we could not, as a species or as individuals, possibly do without. But neither if we are to remain sane, can we possibly do without direct perception."

F. S. C. NORTHROP:
> "The culture of the United States is initiating a shift to a new philosophical foundation...rooted in the intuitive esthetic component (which) is immediately apprehensible and the theoretic component (which) is scientifically verifiable...The good society of the world must combine (them)."

CONTENTS

PART IV
REASON

PART V
WHOLENESS

Grateful acknowledgement to authors and publishers for permission to quote from their books appears in the *Appendix*.

Superior numbers throughout the text refer to corresponding reference numbers in *Appendix* showing the source of material.

PART I

DESPAIR

IMMANUEL KANT:
"Man wishes concord, but nature knows better what is good for his species; and she wills discord: in order that man may be impelled to a new exertion of his powers, and to further development of his natural capacities."

CHAPTER 1

DISILLUSIONMENT

PREVIEW

Is there no dormant good or love of others inherent in all men waiting to be awakened?

On the answer to this question may depend the survival of the human race. If the answer is no, mankind seems doomed to self-destruction — atomic — ethical — or worse.

Or are there ways to arouse man's deeper better self — if any?

This awakening to the good in himself, in his fellow men, and the universe, can be **induced** by any of the six higher religions — especially if revivified by modern psychologies. Or it can be **induced** by psychology — usually Jungian but sometimes Freudian.

Or it can be **spontaneous** — as in the case of poets (Whitman, Millay, Emerson, and Dante) and saints and some of us who are neither — like me.

Methods may vary but results are remarkably alike. A joyous release of the person's ethical, loving, intuitive, spiritual self, of the latent love for his fellow men, desire to serve them, and a feeling of communication with the creative principle of the universe. If the process is complete, his Reason unites with his Feeling and Intuition to create the whole man. Only the whole man can create the good life for the individual and the good society for all in this age of Science and Materialism.

If this renaissance of the deeper part of man's personality became sufficiently prevalent, might it not bring permanent peace to a disastrously warring world? Everything else has failed.

THE FIVE STEPS

Whatever the method — religious, psychological, or spontaneous — mature perception of the nature of man, the universe, and his relation to it usually is precipitated, paradoxically enough, by suffering — if deep enough. In fact, to develop his highest potentialities, man apparently must obey certain mysterious laws of the human psyche and climb five difficult psychological steps: Despair, "Death," Rebirth, Reason, and Wholeness.

RELIGION

If man's awakening to the good is induced by organized religion, Arnold Toynbee informs us that the first three steps are fundamentally the same in all the six higher disciplines: Hinduism, Judaism, Islam, Christianity, Zoroastrianism, and Buddhism (Hinayana and Mahayana). In his *Historian's Approach to Religion*, he describes it as an encounter first with suffering, then the "giving-up of self-centeredness"[1] (which feels like death), and "communication with the presence behind the phenomena"[2] (or rebirth whose aftermath is love of others and desire to serve them and the cosmic principle).

Some deeply religious persons have been content to stop after achieving these three stages and not continue through stages four and five. Today however many demand the rational explanations supplied by modern psychology and philosophy.

PSYCHOLOGY

If man's "self-realization"[3] is evoked by Jungian psychology — which is designed for normal persons as well as neurotic — all five steps are involved. But even in the normal person, Jung says, some form of suffering initiates the transformation. Then comes "the dissolution of the ego in the [collective] unconscious, a state resembling death."[4]

Next, that strange psychological law "the reversal of the opposites"[5] goes into operation. Temporary "death" of his conscious mind eventually is transformed into a rebirth by the release of man's collective unconscious, dwelling place of his ethical, esthetic, intuitive, creative self.

Finally his Reason or conscious mind must understand and accept the contents (good and evil) of his deeper unconscious. Thus he is made into the complete man as nature intended. Jungian therapy often leads to a religious experience but Jung warns that scientifically this is "no proof of the existence of a God."[6] He maintains, however, that today's world-wide sickness is due to the dissociation of man's conscious mind (or Reason) from his collective unconscious (or Feeling and Intuition) — home of his spiritual heritage.

Many heretofore meaningless biblical clichés become psychologically credible through Jung. "He that loseth his life shall find it."[7] "Unless a man (die and) be born again he cannot see the kingdom of God."[8]

Dr. Ira Progoff in his *Death and Rebirth of Psychology* informs us that Freud, despite his original strictures against all religion, admitted in later life that the psychologists must delve deeper into man than the "personal unconscious," seat of neuroses. They must awaken his deeper creative unconscious.[9]

Certainly one of the chief characteristics of a neurosis is the inability to love. One of the chief characteristics of a genuine awakening is a genuine love of humanity. So Freudian therapy is needed to remove obstructions in the path that lead to a cosmic consciousness.

Also it is necessary to know a man's type of physique as this determines his temperament according to the Constitutional psychologist, Dr. William Sheldon.

POETRY

If the liberation of man's joyous intuitive insights into "the Good, the True, and the Beautiful" is spontaneous and poetic, he may not pass through all the five stages — though of course he may seek scientific verification. The records of the poets are beautiful but not complete.

In *Renascense*,* Edna Millay describes her own "death"[10] and burial under six feet of earth,[11] her rebirth[12] through "a miracle of orchard breath,"[13] communion with the spirit of the universe, and her love of all suffering mankind.

In *Leaves of Grass*, Whitman exhibits only the results of his great mystical awakening at thirty-four: his overwhelming love of the world and everybody and everything in it with only brief references to a higher power.

In *The Divine Comedy*, Dante traces his own painful psychological and spiritual journey through Purgatory and Hades and his final arrival at the radiant blinding light which is Heaven — states which he experienced at the age of thirty-five and later disguised and projected as allegory.

That otherwise puzzling masterpiece of poetic prose, Bunyan's *Pilgrim's Progress*, is illuminated by Dr. Esther Harding in *Journey Into Self*. She traces the parallels between the states of spontaneous awakening of the poetic mind and Jungian therapy. Both obey the same irrevocable laws of the human psyche.

I am no poet alas! That probably is the reason I passed through all five stages: Despair, Death, Rebirth, Reason, and Wholeness. But my renascence was gloriously spontaneous and it felt poetic. I can take no credit for it. I was so ignorant I did not have the faintest idea what was happening to me. I merely allowed nature her wonders to perform. Why are we rational scientific moderns afraid to listen to the voice of nature, our own inner nature? We have nothing to lose but our despair.

One day, despite a happy personal life, I suddenly drowned in the sea of my own despair concerning the political chaos of the world and the ethical deterioration of the human race of today. I "died" because men's destruction

*From *Renascence and Other Poems*, Harper & Brothers, Copyright © 1912, 1940 by Edna St. Vincent Millay.

of the peace of the world seemed to prove man was innately evil.

To save myself I instituted a search for the inborn good in man — if any. This unavoidably became a search for the intrinsic good in myself — if any. And in turn this evolved into an unconscious search for the ultimate good in the universe — if any.

As an answer to my quest, I was visited by rare moments of exaltation a-roused by sea and sun and wind, by the ennobling power of great music, the purifying principle of fine painting, the liberating force of poetry, by thinking a thought, even dancing a dance. Enlightening moments when I had flashes of intuitive insight into the nature of things. Illuminating moments when I united — or seemed to — with Ultimate Reality — if there was such a thing. I was reborn.

As a result I suddenly loved the whole world — momentarily, longed to sacrifice my life for others — temporarily, partook briefly of a Good infinitely greater than myself — it seemed.

But our scientific culture of the West scoffs at such irrationalities however beautiful. My own Reason rejected them all unless I could verify them by science. I couldn't. So I plunged into years of intense research in philosophy from Plato to Kant, to Bergson, to Emerson, to Northrop; in the rival psychologies of Freud, Jung, Sheldon, James, Bucke, and Huxley; in comparative religion, and the pro-founder poets. Who was correct?

Finally the answer was found and one day my Reason united with my In-tuition and Feeling and I was made whole. But how could this kind of awaken-ing to the Good be brought to others?

Must the psychologies of tomorrow incorporate the spiritual experiences of man in their systems — or fail? Must the religion of tomorrow incorporate the modern psychologies in their systems — or fail? Would pioneer organiza-tions like the Academy of Religion and Mental Health succeed in the coordina-tion of psychology and religion?

Perhaps my personal experience might throw a little light on our universal problem — the awakening of rational scientific man to the dormant half of his personality — the loving, ethical, esthetic, intuitive, spiritual self. It reveals the unsuspected treasures in us all.

THE STORY

One morning I awakened dreading to face another day unaware that despair — if deep enough — sometimes brings ecstasy. It was Christmas day, 1949 — the day which was to change my entire life.

The thump of the newspaper had awakened me as the delivery boy hurled it against the front door. I lay there asking myself, what new world crisis will the headlines fling in our faces today? The papers had served tragedy with every American breakfast every morning for the last ten years. Six years of death and destruction and horror in the Nazis' World War II. Then four years of argument pro and con in the Communist cold war. How much more could the poor bewildered battered human race endure without cracking up?

Wearily I rose and took my shower. It failed to give me that old accustomed sensuous pleasure. Nothing did any more. My despair about the political chaos of the world and the ethical decline of modern man increased steadily — despite a happy marriage, beloved home, and modest success in my profession. Private happiness was not enough. Nowadays most of us cared about the destiny of the human race with every fiber of our being.

Laconically I brushed my hair as I sat at the dressing table. I stared at the image in the mirror. Is this, I demanded, that Utopian world men in their infinite wisdom promised waiting trusting women? Two world wars in one lifetime and the daily threat of a third? Have men brought the good life to the individual or the good society to all as they so loudly proclaimed they would?

But this was Christmas day. I must not allow my depression to cloud the holiday for the other members of my household. I put on my lipstick and tied a bright red ribbon around my hair. Perhaps that would distract their attention from the dark circles under my sleepless eyes. But who could sleep?

Already the scientists had offered us a solution to all the problems of mankind — complete annihilation by the atomic bomb. That was not quite the solution we sought. But America had used it tragically on Hiroshima. And only this September Russia also had discovered the atom bomb. Now it hung like the sword of Damocles, it hung by a whim over the heads of every man, woman, and child on the face of the earth. Atomic fear by night and despair by day. How would it all end?

Already the newspapers were discussing the possibility of the human race living underground. If we had regressed that far, why live at all? I wouldn't want to certainly.

I slipped on my red and gold housecoat and slowly descended the stairs. My husband already was in the dining room. He rose and gallantly drew out my chair even after all these years of marriage. We kissed good morning and wished each other a Merry Christmas.

Usually the bright colors of our Eighteenth Century interior warmed my heart against the mad modern world. But today I did not even see the Adam-green paneling, the long sweep of the red damask draperies, or the crystal chandeliers which tinkled at every footstep. My eyes flew apprehensively to the New York paper the maid already had placed on the stand before my husband's plate.

He invariably urged me not to read it until after breakfast. My distressed comments distracted his mind from his day's business and upset my digestion.

"Honestly, my dear," he often said, "you aren't Atlas. You can't take the weight of the whole world on your shoulders without being crushed yourself. But every cruelty in Asia seems to pain you. Every discord in Europe disturbs you. Every injustice in America sickens you. It isn't all your responsibility."

"Isn't it everyone's responsibility?"

It seemed unwise, however, to tell him that every morning for the last few weeks — or was it months — the unremitting world crises in the headlines turned my breakfast to a hard cold lump, made my heart race with frightening noise, and my hands become pieces of ice. Tension was tying my whole body in knots.

I rang for the cook and second maid. They entered smiling broadly. My husband distributed his envelopes of Christmas money first, then my gifts to them lying under the small tree. They opened them amid much laughter. We all wished each other Merry Christmas and Happy New Year many times, then they returned to the kitchen.

While waiting for our breakfasts we unwrapped the tall pile of books beside each of our plates. We never gave anything but books — all selected by me — at the instigation of my husband.

Then the maid brought in a stack of hot cakes. I smothered the golden brown beauties in good ole Texas molasses. All my life I had enjoyed a keen zest for delicious food. I tasted them. They had no flavor. The syrup had lost its sweetness. Life itself had completely lost its former sweetness.

Day after day for years I had expected some respite from the proofs of man's steady deterioration. Month after month I hoped for cheerful news in the morning paper of his sudden renascence. Hope deferred certainly made my heart too sick for words.

Finally my husband passed the morning paper over to me. "No world catastrophies this morning to devastate you," he said smiling. "So I won't have to worry about you for one day at least."

I smiled at him but stared incredulously at the banner headline: "Peace on earth, good will toward men."

How dared they, I thought. The effrontery. The hypocrisy! The tragic irony of it. There was no peace anywhere and even less good will. Hatred filled the air of half the nations of the globe like poison gas. Never had the human race witnessed anything quite like it. It was sickening. And what was being done about it? What could be done about it?

Many of our most brilliant intellectuals worshipped Science as omnipotent, Reason as omniscient, and benevolent Politics and Economics as the best panacea for the ills of the world and of the individual. And I had worshipped the intellectuals. The benefits of these four disciplines were obvious. But today reason itself announced that the day of reckoning was come at last.

Had politics prevented world wars? Or materialism abolished man's inhumanity to man? Had science prevented diabolical destruction? Or reason taught man to love his fellow men as himself? Had organized religions brought peace to the earth in 3,000 years?

Mankind had tried anything. Everything had failed disastrously. The world was rushing toward its own senseless doom — atomic — ethical — or worse. The situation was hopeless, the individual helpless.

My grief at the tragic state of affairs was like a pail too full of water. It required only one more drop to make it overflow dangerously. Today somehow, I did not know why, those seven innocent little words, "Peace on earth, good will toward men," furnished that final fatal drop.

Suddenly as I sat there at the breakfast table playing with my uneaten food, I could feel it physically as all the fight drained out of my body like water through a sieve.

I could feel the mainspring of my life which had been wound tighter and tighter by anxiety about world conditions for ten terrible years now quietly break. This was it. This was the end. I had finally reached the breaking point. The catastrophe I had feared for so long had struck. I must seek privacy before I collapsed and disgraced myself.

I glanced at my husband reading the second edition of the paper. How soon did I dare leave the table without alarming him?

Finally he rose and left the dining room carrying his Christmas books. I sat on stupefied, forgetting to ring for the maid to clear the table. I barely escaped before she entered. She must not be allowed to witness my distress.

I tried to rise but suddenly my body had become incredibly heavy. I dragged myself out to the hall and like a woman a thousand years old pulled myself by the bannisters up the stairs. Laboriously I climbed on up to my little sanctuary on the floor above. My work room was on the quiet third floor of our quiet house in Connecticut.

For years it had been my custom to write here every morning from nine to one without household interruptions — presumably. Writing had been impossible for months. The creative stream which had flowed so freely for years now was mysteriously frozen at its source. How could anyone write anything when all human values were deteriorating in bewildering fashion right under our very eyes?

Stupidly I fumbled with the lock, then I entered and fell like a dead weight onto the old blue couch where in happier days I had lain to correct my typed manuscripts. I had published a novel, magazine articles, and a few radio plays. Today I lay there face down prostrated by the enormous weight of this one last straw.

Month after month I had sat in this room playing hungrily with the typewriter keys, struggling desperately, hopelessly, to **think** my way out of my despair. This was the age of Reason, wasn't it? If rational thought could not solve our problems — universal and personal — what could, in heaven's name?

Reason, however, had proved to be nothing but a merciless searchlight. It revealed with glaring clarity certain hideous facts hitherto comfortably vague. Today I turned its powerful beam once again over the events of the last ten years. Suddenly I beheld for the first time a horrifying truth.

For ideals many misguided men had attempted **deliberately** to destroy the ethical values and moral standards which had sustained the human race for centuries! Honor. Honesty. Compassion! Self-reliance! Justice. But above all the love of freedom!

No, no, no, I wailed inwardly closing my eyes against the fearful sight. These were the foundations on which America, the whole Western world, had built itself into greatness — on which I had constructed my whole life.

Men's behavior all over the world in the last ten years had proved **men did not want freedom.** They wanted security even at the price of submission under Fascist or Communist dictatorships. The shock of this discovery stunned me. I had been brought up under the precepts of Thomas Jefferson. My father had quoted him to me constantly. And I too had sworn "eternal vigilance against tyranny over the minds of men." Freedom, Jefferson said, was man's most precious possession. But how could you fight to give men something they did not even want?

All my life I had fought for freedom for myself and others — freedom from the pressures of the home, the school, the church, society, custom, tradition, and conventions. Was everything I had ever done now valueless? And without a hierarchy of values would we not all be lost like rudderless ships?

Now inexorable logic pointed its awful finger at the last awful truth. Men's wars and bombs of the last decade, wholesale death and destruction, deception and gullibility, their criminal apathy and unprecedented cruelty proved just one thing: **Man is inherently evil!**

No, no, **No!** I moaned aloud. I recoiled physically from the blow. I clutched the couch in desperate fingers. I had been brought up to believe in the innate good in man. But now —

I held my breath. I closed my eyes. Cold sickness invaded me like silent water rising ominously in a well. Now the last remaining fragment of my faith in mankind disappeared forever. Without this faith I had no support under my life. Did not our beliefs constitute the house in which we lived and moved and had our being? Without it, would we not be swept away in a chaotic flood? Certainly without this faith in mankind, life was scarcely worth the living. I could not live in a hideous world of evil men and women. No one could.

Yet somehow I felt strangely numb. All during these last ten years of worldwide turmoil and anxiety, my emotions had responded too often, too intensely, to too many international crises. Now I could feel nothing. My will to live was quietly ebbing away like the last waves when the tide runs out.

This was the most awful day of my entire life.

I turned my face to the wall and waited. For what? The end? A quiet death? I did not know. I did not care.

But I had no idea of what was happening to me. I never had heard at this time of William James' theory of psychological death, "the dying to be truly born."[14]

All my life, however, I had heard the old biblical cliche, "He that loses his life shall find it."[15] I did not believe a word of it. I did not understand it might be a profound psychological truth.

PART II

"DEATH"

EDNA ST. VINCENT MILLAY, Renascence:*
"No hurt I did not feel, no death
That was not mine...
All suffering mine...
Ah, awful weight!
And so beneath the weight lay I
And suffered death, but could not die."[1]

*From *Renascence and Other Poems,* Harper & Brothers, Copyright © 1912, 1940 by Edna St. Vincent Millay.

CHAPTER 2

THE UNKNOWN SEA

DROWNING

Stricken motionless, I lay there on the old blue couch in my work room — waiting. Great waves of desolation washed over me. For ten years I had struggled daily to keep my head above water, to save myself from drowning in the sea of my own despair. Now like an exhausted swimmer, I was too weary even to save my own life.

I could feel a leaden weight on my back, the realization of man's evil nature. It was dragging me down — down. I sank deeper and deeper through the fathomless black waters of defeat.

I felt on the verge of blacking out, of losing consciousness. Now I knew I was dying! I did not care. I did not resist. It was an indescribable sensation. A horrible cessation of sweet life. A taste of the bitter waters of futility. A being weighed down by dead dreams and false hopes. The end of all movement, all thought, all hope. The death of sensation. A terrifying nothingness.

I struck bottom. I lay there motionless at the bottom of the world like some heavy water-soaked object. Inert. Insensible. Unconscious. **Dead!**

Minutes, hours, a thousand years passed — or so it seemed. Time became timeless.

Gradually the consciousness which I doubt very much I ever had lost completely, commenced to return. With no effort on my part I was floated up to the surface of life again from this deep sea of oblivion. I was flung painfully back onto the rough shore of consciousness.

I lay there motionless like a spent swimmer on the sands. I was too unspeakably weary — indifferent — sore — to move. My physical body felt bruised as if it had been beaten and battered by angry pounding waves. The sight of purple marks on my flesh would not have surprised me one iota. I rested precariously on the dangerous shore of this terrible sea of desolation.

But nature moves in mysterious ways her wonders to perform. Finally I opened my eyes. I knew I would live. But what horrible calamity had befallen me? I did not know. But I did know that nature helps those who help themselves.

I must do something drastic to prevent being swept out to sea again. I felt frightened — desperate. I looked about me. How could I save myself? My wits scrambled to their feet.

Apparently I had "died" psychologically from despair at the evil behavior of modern man which proved his evil nature. Then could I save myself now by instituting a search for the inherent good in man — if any? Could he be judged not by his **overt actions** but by his **inborn nature**? Were they two separate parts or the same?

I grasped the sides of the couch convulsively. I said to myself, I must reexamine not what man by his own efforts has **done** to wreck the peace of the world but what he intrinsically **is**. What is the **inner** man really like? I had no idea.

In fear and desperation I clasped my hands passionately together. Has he no perennial clarity of vision? No deathless hierarchy of ethical values? No infallible inner guide to right and wrong? Is man nothing but a helpless leaf to be blown willy nilly in any direction by any winds of doctrine — good or ill? Has he no deep tap roots in the good earth to anchor him in political storms, to nourish him in time of moral drought?

On the answers to such questions might depend my very life and perhaps the future fate of the human race. There was no answer.

I rose heavily and plodded slowly around the battered and beloved old desk. I must search into the hidden-most depths of human nature. But how? I must probe the representative of mankind I knew best. But whom?

I looked in appeal at the many books making colored mosaics against my study wall. Frantically I attempted to probe to the depths of a dozen world-famous people I admired. No, it was impossible.

For the first time in my life books had failed me in a moment of dire need. I went to the window. I leaned my hot forehead against the cold glass pane. I stared out blindly at the driving snow. Whom could I examine for possible inherent good?

Finally the answer struck me like a blow in my face. That person must unavoidably be — myself! Oh, no, no! I felt too unworthy. After all I was merely an average worldly woman leading an average worldly life. Certainly no model of virtue, no shining representative of the human race.

I turned and paced slowly up and down the floor. I had no choice — if I wanted to be saved from recurring despair.

My body was so exhausted from its harrowing experience of "drowning"

I fell once again into the chair at the desk. Hopelessly I pounded my stupid forehead with my fists. I must think, think!

Anxiously I reviewed my life. Yes, I could recall a few instances when I seemed to exhibit a little forbearance and kindness toward other people above the call of justice. But no, on closer scrutiny these all proved to be magnanimity cloaking self-interest.

Frightened — frenzied — my thoughts began to dash this way and that like animals in a cage. Was there no way out?

THE SEARCH BEGINS

I sank hopelessly again onto the old blue couch. Was there no intrinsic good in this representative of humanity lying prostrate on the couch and therefore in all mankind?

Now I searched not my outward actions but my inner being. No, I could find no inborn good buried even in the remotest corners of myself. None. So I was doomed to permanent despair!

Then suddenly mysterious incidents in my past emerged like shining peaks above the prevailing grey fog. Strange beautiful frightening incidents which had been visited upon me unsought — unexpected — and were usually unwelcome.

All my life I had had experiences I was too ignorant to understand. Our materialistic scientific Western Culture scoffed at such irrational episodes. I feared they meant I was queer — or worse. Consequently I always had buried them in the darkest corner of my memory.

Rapturous incidents like the time I ran in the wild Texas wind and that fearful delicious thing happened. Like that day in the Alabama coal mine when I saw my kindergarten children "trailing clouds of glory."[2] And once when I wrote a book and was "blasted with excess of light."[3] Once when I was kissed and was dazzled by seeing the face of the unseeable. There were a dozen more.

What was that mysterious element which pervaded these ecstatic moments like an elusive light? Could "It" possess any ultimate value? What was It? And could It save me now?

Certainly not, my reason protested, promptly rejecting them. But some strange instinctive compulsion beyond reason urged me on.

I sighed heavily. I was too exhausted to think any more, to care any more. Let come what may.

Weary beyond belief I lay there inert on the writing couch in my study, all defenses down, abnormally quiet, unable to move, undesirous of moving ever again so long as I lived. Yet in some unfathomable way beyond my feeble comprehension, my psychological "death"[4] had released me from ten years of terrible tension.

Now I could feel myself softly cushioned in the warm luxury of my own relaxed nerves. Like a great cat lying in the sun. I had stopped fighting. (I had reached that point of complete abandonment James and Jung say is essential for rebirth, as I was to learn later.)

Then suddenly another extraordinary thing was visited upon me without so much as by your leave. It was so vivid, so real, it was a physical sensation. I felt the door of my inmost self being opened wide automatically. It was like those modern doors controlled by rays of an electronic "eye." It made me hold my breath in fear — joy — awe. Now there flowed forth a mighty subterranean stream. It rose from unknown depths within me. A river of memory. "It was a miracle of rare device."[5] I lay there overwhelmed — incredulous — frightened — waiting — waiting —

Now the very antithesis of the Freudian process seemed to be occurring without my volition. Always I had assumed, erroneously, that the unconscious mind was a muddy reservoir containing nothing except neurotic miseries. I never had read that neuroses were only in people's "personal unconscious"[6] and that Jung had discovered remoter layers of our normal healthy "collective unconscious,"[7] a deep sea of buried treasures.

Suddenly my forgotten joys began to pour forth in a clear sparkling stream — the concealed, repressed, most ecstatic incidents of my entire life. Paradoxically enough, they poured forth from me yet I felt as if I were floating along on this stream of memory — being carried swiftly, helplessly, willingly — I knew not where.

Periodically poor proud Reason struggled feebly to stem this mysterious flood, fearful of the unwelcome truths it might uncover. What truths? I did not know but they seemed to be lurking dangerously just below the surface.

Nevertheless an irresistible compulsion urged me on. Some deep inner voice warned me to abandon myself to this exploration of the unknown region in my deepest self. I must trust my instinct. I had tried everything else. Everything else had failed me — especially Reason which now finally became submerged completely beneath this rushing river of memory.

From this minute on, I felt as if some external power beyond my control like radar guided me — to what distant goal I could not even surmise.

And every morning thereafter I withdrew to my sanctuary on the third floor. There I allowed that exciting frightening process to continue of its own momentum while I floated in a deliciously somnambulant state — a passive instrument being used by nature — or whatever.

Thus began a gradual awakening, a slow rebirth, so rich, so full, it was to require a whole glorious incredible year to run its course. Soon I was to relive chronologically in vivid detail some twenty ecstatic experiences from my past life. Formerly discarded and discredited, they now were revivified and intensified threefold. They streaked like meteors across the dark night of my despair. They illuminated the latent good, the love, the truth I was unaware existed in me and in all human beings. For no one is unique.

So one after the other I lived again through those rare moments of exaltation I had known all my life but dismissed. Moments aroused spontaneously by sea and sun and wind, by the purifying power of fine painting, the ennobling principle in great music, the fructifying force of poetry, by thinking a thought, even dancing a dance. Enlightening moments when I felt I had flashes of intuitive insight into the eternal verities. Illuminating moments when I united — or seemed to — with a radiant blinding light of some vast cosmic force — if there was such a thing — which my Reason always had denied hotly as untenable.

Thus began my search for the good in man — if any. This unavoidably became a desperate search for the good in myself — if any. Later this in turn evolved into an unconscious search for the good in the universe — if any.

It was that eternal search of man for what the philosophers call Ultimate Reality. The quest which comes inevitably when the world is at its ethical worst as it is today and the individual in his deepest despair as he is today. A search that comes to some of us involuntarily through ecstasy.

It is an ecstasy which, however, may be aroused in all of us in varying degree by the seven natural stimuli: **art** — if great enough; **nature** when beautiful enough; **love** — if deep enough; **passion** — when high enough; **thought** — if sufficiently intense; **relaxation** — if complete; and the rhythmic **motion** of our muscles if they are mesomorphic enough.

Soon I was to discover an old secret known long ago by the dervishes in their holy whirling, by American Indians and other primitive peoples whose dances aroused their spiritual consciousness. For the rhythmic motion of our own mesomorphic muscles can remove the invisible barrier to our own profounder nature and permit the stream of infinite good to flow through us.

Or was it merely the wind which initiated my awakening?

PART III

REBIRTH THROUGH ECSTASY

CHAPTER 3

WIND

It all began in Texas that day of the Great Norther.

It was the first of those strange beautiful frightening experiences which were to change my whole life eventually.

Suddenly the shutters commenced to bang violently. The windows rattled like things demented. The servants ran all over the house laughing like excited children struggling to close the doors and windows. It was a warm sunny Autumn day — the kind a Norther always preferred.

I was lying on the floor reading fairy tales — my head in the clouds, my nose in a book — an acrobatic feat of which my mother complained frequently. Too frequently.

A cold gust of wind swept through the room turning the pages of my book with quick invisible fingers without as much as by your leave.

I leapt up and dashed eagerly out of the house. My mother stopped me. She and my father were standing on the front porch watching the wild cavortings of the North wind with disgusting calm.

"Now, Sugar Plum," she admonished me, "don't run too hard in the wind today or I'll have Pearl put you to bed without any supper."

Never would she commit such a colossal crime! She knew I loved eating better than anything in the world — except running in the wind and reading and school and boys and pretty red hair ribbons.

Quickly I fled on out into our overgrown old Southern garden to greet my favorite playmate, the wind. But today everything looked too different, too unnatural. It was frightening. I stood in the center of this wildly agitated garden — motionless.

Today all the trees and bushes created a tumultuously waving green world on every side. This invisible power in the air lifted the great green boughs, waved them, swayed them, bent them almost to the ground. Then they flung up their heads high again half in protest, half in pleasure it seemed, resilient beyond belief.

It seized the dark green leaves, tossed them madly, shook them, turned them upside down until their pale undersides were revealed.

I continued to stand there hypnotized. My fascinated eyes followed the wind's other sleight-of-hand tricks. It passed quickly along the flower beds, stripped the flowers bare of every petal, every leaf, with one careless gesture, leaving the stalks naked and shivering.

The great Norther rushed on laughing, blew new life into the dead leaves sleeping peacefully under the bushes, drove them in a frenzied race across the green grass, rolled them over and over on edge like small brown wheels, halted them abruptly, whirled them up higher into the air with lordly abandon, then deserted them to fall safely back to earth as best they might.

What a Norther! The most violent I ever had seen.

Suddenly a colder bolder gust blew its breath in my face, ran icy fingers through my hair, whipped my dress about my bony young knees. My gingham skirt snapped like the crack of a whip, tugging at me to join in this wild Autumn bacchanal.

Now I felt stunned by that unearthly roar of the wind through the trees, frightened by the strange sound the frantic fluttering leaves made. Like hundreds of small green hands beating together hysterically.

Suddenly a bubbling spring of mysterious joy welled up inside me. I commenced to run, to race with the wind, against the wind, over the green grass, over the flower beds, between the madly swaying bushes. I flung my arms up. My long thin legs moved as awkwardly as a colt's. I laughed aloud in the face of those frightened white clouds. Swiftly they rushed across the blue sky under the long lash of that ruthless North wind.

"I'm not afraid like those stupid ole clouds! I love the wind. It's the best playmate in the world. Better than any girl or rough ole boy."

Faster and faster I danced. For once I was free. Free to be my natural animal self. Free from my mother's daily don'ts. From the satin-lined prison of ladylike decorum. No arms at sides, voice lowered, walk sedate, joy moderated.

Free from the admonishing voices of teachers — day and Sunday. And from the sin I never felt but ministers said I must.

So on and on I raced.

The wind respected nothing. It snatched my beloved red ribbon from my hair, caught the ends of my long curls, lashed them across my face like sharp whips stinging my cheeks. I loved it! Pain only increased my pleasures.

Stung into a delicious frenzy, I flung myself with renewed vigor into this orgy. Never had I felt so ecstatically happy in my life! Why? I did not know. I did not care.

Mind you, a Norther is not a storm. It is a freak of nature. A cold streak of wind. It does not rain. It blows. It cuts through a warm sunny day like a sharp knife through a ripe melon. It is incredibly sudden, brief and exciting. It is gone almost before it arrives. You never forget it — if you were ever ten in Texas.

My inner ear listened for that mysterious message. The North wind was a tantalizing voice calling me to fairer fields of fulfillment. But where? I did not know. But it promised impossible delights. Why, I did not know. I suddenly commenced to turn around and around in giddy circles. Faster and faster I gyrated with all the fervor of a whirling young dervish.

My own momentum carried me on and on. I was so dizzy I could scarcely stand. The rhythmic motion of my own muscles, the sight of those wildly agitated trees, the roar of the wind, whipped me into an exultation too delicious to endure.

That was when it happened.

That incredible, indescribable wonder.

Suddenly without the slightest warning I felt different. Did I continue dancing or had I already stopped? I shall never know. My physical body — till now so warm and real seemed to be melting right away. Like a lump of sugar in a cup of hot tea.

Now I felt the tug of some mysterious force drawing me — irresistibly — toward what? Black blank annihilation? I was afraid, mortally afraid. And I resented this violation of my privacy without so much as a by your leave. Yet it was a wonderful sensation too. Like that last voluptuous moment before losing consciousness when you are under gas at the dentist's. Was it oblivion? I wanted to resist it. Was it a blissful nothingness? I wanted to surrender.

Abruptly the visible world about me vanished as if by magic. I lost all awareness of where I was. And time — there was no time. There was nothing left in the entire universe except this mysterious power preying on me and my little hard gold nugget of consciousness resisting it. I was still holding on to that for dear life. What was happening to me? Was I dying? Or losing my mind?

Now this seductive force invaded my inmost being. Now that last little hard core, the very kernel of my being, commenced to dissolve, to be absorbed by this inexorable force. Was it the wind drawing me magnetically into itself? Was I becoming part of the mighty currents of the Norther?

All personal identity vanished. I was no longer I. I did not exist. Yet I did exist. I seemed to have existed for countless ages in the past and into the future. But there was no past, no future, only this dark warm present.

I felt suspended in vibrant space — in timeless time.

Then for one terrible blissful moment I felt as if — as if I had merged indivisibly with the wind. **I was the wind!**

Frightened, ecstatic, I felt my truest self magically released for the first time in my life. This was not the polite obedient little girl adults forced me to be.

It was myself. It felt good — good! It was no one I had known existed. Now my inner self felt purified, freed from some unknown bondage...

All hungers fed...all loneliness comforted...all questions answered...Now, if not forever.

How long this strange, painful, delicious sensation continued I do not know. A minute. A year. They seemed the same.

Finally fear saved me from what I mistook to be the threat of permanent dissolution. Human fear stabbed me back to consciousness again like a long cold knife thrust into a sleeping man. I stood there in the center of the garden — dazed, frightened out of my wits, my body throbbing as if I had a hundred hearts, my cheeks burning like twin flames.

At least I had returned to consciousness, if indeed I ever had lost it. I was relieved to be safely back on solid earth again. Instinctively I felt the need of seeking reassurance in good warm human contact. Slowly on trembling legs I walked back toward the house.

"Go away, Mr. Wind, go away," I said. "I'm happy enough without you. What with boys and school and red hair ribbons and chocolate candy and everything. Besides you had no right to come bothering me without even asking me if I wanted you."

I tiptoed up the front steps still panting violently, my eyes cast down to conceal my fearful secret from prying eyes. I hoped to gain the privacy of my own room without being observed.

My mother whirled around.

"Look at the chile! Her face is positively purple. Now young lady, march yourself straight to the bathroom and dash cold water on your face. You're not going to have any supper. And don't expect ole Liza to smuggle you in milk toast or anything either."

As I opened the screen door, she turned back to my father. "I declare, I don't know what we're going to do with that chile. She studies too hard. Even plays too hard. I simply don't understand her. She's too intense about everything. What **will** become of her!"

CHAPTER 4

THINKING

One Sunday afternoon I was sitting on the side porch reading assiduously. Three boys came strolling along the quiet sidewalk and halted. They were in my class in High School. I was about fourteen, I think.

They called my name, whistled, made jokes. With all my strength I resisted the temptation to talk to them. I kept my eyes religiously on my book. But I no longer knew what I was reading.

Finally the boldest of the three stepped blithely into my mother's precious nasturtium bed. He jumped up on the porch and straddled the bannister. I still pretended to be oblivious to the entire male sex and absorbed in my book.

"Take it, Clairene. They're chocolates," he said, extending the small paper bag toward me.

Now I loved chocolate candy better than anything in the world except perhaps the admiration of boys. I ignored his offering. Promptly the boys ate the candy themselves. My mouth watered.

Now the leader of the group tiptoed across the gallery and glanced at the large black book spread on my lap. "Great jumping Jehosaphat! It's the Holly Bibble she's a-readin'! Run for your life, fellers!"

And run they did, all of them. The first boys who ever had called on me in my life. Now I had lost them. I was heartbroken. The goal of every Southern girl was to be a belle, to be besieged by boys day and night. Never would they come again. I felt extremely virtuous — and unhappy.

I had set myself the stupendous task of reading the Bible from cover to cover. What more appropriate day than Sunday? But why was it so unintelligible, so uninteresting with all its long lists of "begats"? Certain chapters, however, sang like music but I really could not understand a word of any of it.

The following Sunday afternoon I carried my book to the back porch. I feared I might succumb to the temptation of talking to the boys if they should come again. To my amazement the same three boys appeared at the back screen door. I never suspected the fine maternal hand in the plot.

They scratched against the screen wire like puppies, barked, and whimpered to be admitted. It was almost impossible to suppress my laughter. I prayed for strength to resist them. Eventually they strolled away laughing at their rebuff with a callowness that shocked and hurt me.

The third Sunday I was certain the boys would not call again. A golden opportunity any girl would covet had been missed. Nevertheless I sat out on the front porch rocking violently to show the whole world I was *not* reading any book. This drastic change in my attitude toward the Bible and boys had evolved during the intervening week. Several catastrophies had occurred.

Today however to my delight the three brave knights returned reinforced by a fourth recruit and armed with sheet music of the popular songs of the day. They stood uncertainly on the sidewalk. I smiled my best smile. Shyly the four boys straggled up the steps.

My parents suddenly appeared from nowhere. I introduced the boys. My mother suggested that I telephone three other girls to rush right over. They soon arrived. Then the eight of us spent a hilarious Sunday afternoon — the first of many — eating everything in sight, laughing at nothing, and singing loudly to my very sketchy piano playing.

Those disturbing episodes, however, between the second and third week had begun with my first kiss. I had read George Eliot's *Adam Bede*, convinced that I should become a woman minister the instant I grew up. My first kiss, however, cast doubt on my vocation.

For one Wednesday evening I had gone to prayer meeting with an older girl and her handsome young cousin. After church we sat in our rose garden in the moonlight. He kissed me lightly on the forehead. This kiss shook the entire moral order of the universe right down to its foundations as far as I was concerned. Had not my mother, all mothers, and all ministers, declared all sex was sinful?

That night I said my prayers with a fervor greater than ever in my life. "Please, God, help me. My father says I must always tell the truth about everything no matter what happens. But if I am honest, I must admit I enjoyed being kissed. So how can you say it's wrong when you make kissing so pleasant, then make us weak enough to give in to it, and then punish us for giving in? Is that fair?"

Conflicts increased internally and externally. One day my father and I were driving home after a long walk together in his favorite woodland.

"Father, lots of people tell me I have the kindest, noblest father in this town. Yet you never go to church. Why?"

"Well," he replied, "I was a deacon in the church for years. I studied my

Bible seriously. But every time I asked my minister the meaning of certain puzzling passages he said he did not know. So I stopped going. But I still have my stenographer read me a chapter in the Bible every day of my life. It's difficult to explain these things to a child. You may wonder, honey, why I tramp in the woods alone so much. Well, to me, the streams and trees and sky form a — a sort of natural cathedral. Someday you may understand."

On the other hand my mother was an ardent church worker. At her behest I attended Sunday school and church regularly. I listened avidly to vehement sermons about the heathen sinners in India and China and Africa and how they would all burn in everlasting hellfires, merely because they were not Christians.

I trembled at the heated exhortations against demon rum, card playing, gambling on the cotton exchange, and dancing. Words like thunderbolts were hurled from the pulpit. We were all conceived in iniquity and born in sin. But of all the evils flesh was heir to, the worst was passion — especially for women — though the resultant motherhood was sacred. A kiss was the first step on the primrose path that led to eternal perdition and brimstone.

Again and again I had sought practical guidance to daily living in the Bible. It was impossible to understand it — at fourteen. My mother gave me a simpler book, "In His Steps." It said that when in doubt all you needed to do was behave as Jesus would have behaved in similar circumstances.

For months I had been attempting to apply it. But would Jesus accept notes from the boys in school? I loved notes. They indicated a girl's popularity. Reluctantly I pushed all notes off the edge of my desk with my elbow as if I had not even noticed them. I must avoid wounding the boy's feelings.

Other unanswerable questions hurled themselves at me thick and fast. Would Jesus eat chocolate candy for sheer physical pleasure? Or wear pretty red hair ribbons which matched his — my, red cheeks? Allow a boy to hold his hand at parties? Read wonderful story books for mere enjoyment that were not school books? Or collect bits of paper containing lines of poetry — words which were not morally exhortatory but so beautiful they laid a spell on you?

Month after month I had struggled unsuccessfully with a child's and an era's misconception of religion. Then shortly before the Sunday when the boys appeared for the third time, the climax had occurred.

One hot Spring afternoon my parents were attending a funeral. It was the hour of the siesta, the time no Southerner in his right mind stirred abroad except in emergency. The servants were asleep out in the servants' house in the back yard. I was supposed to be taking my usual nap in my bedroom. I was in the living room lying on the floor looking at a fascinating book of pictures.

I had the rare pleasure of being alone in the house. The quiet was heavenly. The peace. The privacy. The freedom. I was not reading the Bible. I was not consulting that misleading little grey book *In His Steps*. I had finally decided that if only Jesus had been a girl my problems would have been simpler. I had failed to follow in his footsteps. But why? What was wrong?

I was now studying a forbidden book on anatomy. At least my mother had forbidden it. My father said all knowledge was good. It contained the most extraordinary colored pictures of all the male and female organs — well, not quite all, alas. They folded over each other like paper dolls and could be lifted up separately if you were ever, ever so careful.

Thoughts of God were far removed when suddenly the most terrible storm erupted within me. I trembled with fear and awe. It seemed as if a blasphemous question flashed like lightening across the sky: how do *I* know there is a God?

My heart stood still in an ecstasy of fright. I held my breath waiting to be struck dead for my heresy.

Never had I known any living person who doubted the existence of God. Everybody believed in Him — everybody! Who was little I to doubt what everyone else believed? I was an infidel, a lost sinner.

Now my inner feelings grew so intense they were projected outward until I imagined I saw the earth suddenly rent open in front of me. A great black fathomless chasm leading to hell yawned before me. Like the people in the Bible who were always seeing "visions," I now seemed to see a man spring up out of this awful abyss. He looked exactly like the Devil I had seen in all those Sunday School pictures. A man dressed in red tights with two horns on his head, a long tail, and a trident in his hand.

Surely he had come to carry me off to everlasting Hades for my blasphemy! I thought I could see him dancing about with fiendish glee on the opposite bank. My blood turned to ice water.

I was so dizzy I felt the earth was slipping away. I was falling down, down into endless blackness — perhaps into the everlasting fires of perdition.

After minutes — hours — I did not know which — fear slowly ebbed away. Thank goodness, I was not lost yet. With all the fervor of my trembling young heart, I cried out for help:

"Oh, God, give me a sign that you are there! I cannot take other people's word for it. I must know for myself. I do believe in you, I do! But give me a sign to prove you are there!"

I waited breathless, motionless. At last the answer seemed to come. Silence. A resounding pulsating silence louder than a hundred church bells.

Can reason's rejection of the surface absurdities of any religion pave the way for a genuine spiritual awakening?

CHAPTER 5

MOONLIGHT

At the party that night I danced three times with an inspired dancer. I forgot everything, abandoned myself to the music, melted in the boy's arms until I swam around the room in a delicious sea of sound. It was hypnotic, the rhythmical motion of my own mesomorphic muscles moving to the beat, beat, beat of the drums.

I was home from college for the summer holidays at the delicious age of eighteen.

After such a happy evening my escort and I strolled home reluctantly through the magical world of night. The full moon was riding high in a cloudless sky. This Texas moonlight was golden, warm and yellow. It poured over the whole town drenching the sleeping houses and quiet streets.

We walked as slowly as human feet could move. We strolled under the dark arches formed by the double rows of hackberry trees enclosing the sidewalk on either side. The leaves laid down their patterns of shadow on the white cement. The wind ruffled them gently like black lace as we trod upon them. The soft summer breeze from the Gulf of Mexico caressed our cheeks. The intermittent scent of honeysuckle assaulted our faces like unexpected kisses. The night was perfect. Life was perfect.

Eventually we arrived at our front door. I floated up the stairs on a cloud of happiness. I undressed, then lay in bed gazing out into the moon-soaked garden. That round yellow disk was moving perceptibly down the Western sky. The blazing light shone full in my face. Were the Negroes right? They said if you slept in the moonlight you would become looney.

This subtropical light was thick, yellow, like Jersey cream. You could almost dip it up with your hands. It poured over the garden turning the daytime green of the shrubs, grass, and trees to black. It laid even blacker shadows under the trees like soft round velvet rugs. Intermittently a playful little breeze touched the trees with light fingers then left them trembling with pleasure.

Surely this strange mysterious substance was more than mere light. It flowed into you like some warm golden liquid — expanding, enriching you with inexplicable happiness. But it was **too** beautiful, too overpowering. I closed my eyes to shut it out.

Slowly beauty's twin sister, melancholy, rose up inevitably beside her. It stirred memories of old racial griefs long buried. Suddenly I, who had never consciously known unhappiness in my life, commenced to weep with deep voluptuous pleasure for sorrows I had never known. I felt as though thousands of ancestors for thousands of years were this night weeping through my eyes.

Finally I brushed away the tears impatiently with my bare hands but kept my eyes closed tightly. I refused to look out again at that terrible moonlight. It was too dangerous. My eyes were drawn back magnetically. But now something had gone wrong. The more intently I looked at our familiar garden the more unfamiliar it became. The deeper I gazed into this strange moonlight the stranger it grew. It was hypnotic. I was powerless to turn my eyes away now even if I wished. Gradually the light itself seemed to expand like an opening flower, to shimmer like the distant heat haze on a hot summer's day.

Even the trees appeared different. Not beautiful any longer but mysterious. And how hot it was all of a sudden! That precious little Gulf breeze had died down entirely. A rare occurrence in any Texas summer. And how still it was, how unnaturally silent. No comforting sound of a car. No human footsteps walking abroad this night of the full moon. Not even the usual friendly thud, thud of a frog hopping over the damp earth where old Parker had watered the flower beds at sundown.

Nothing. Not a sound. I was alone in the world with this uncanny moonlight. It was frightening. It was awe-full. Now the whole earth itself seemed to be holding its breath. The trees, the flowers, the very air hung motionless — waiting for something. It was not the stillness of death but of living things. Were they laid under some supernatural spell? All nature waited — but for what?

Mesmerized, I continued to stare against my will at the shrubs, the trees, the moonlight. Suddenly I felt something different emanating from them — an almost sinister coldness. It chilled me. It was as palpable as that cool damp night air rising unexpectedly from the little hollows in the country road. The kind you feel as you ride along on hot summer nights hoping to cool off before going to bed.

What had previously seemed friendly moonlight and green growing things, mere background to personal happiness, were no longer aware of my existence! **Nature was utterly indifferent to me, to all people.** Was such heresy possible! The loss was irreparable. It shook me profoundly.

A nameless fear crept over me. The roots of my hair stirred uneasily on my scalp. Had I been a dog I should have emitted low warning growls.

There was something out there in that garden! I felt it. There was a living thing, a "presence" out there in that moonlight. I tell you I felt it as surely as you feel the presence of a person entering noiselessly behind you in a room.

It was not human exactly. Not animal. Not even supernatural. It was an alien — non-human presence. Not there for the benefit of people. What was it? The spirit of evil peering from behind the skirts of beauty? No, no — it did not **feel** so strong as evil. It felt like — like indifference. That was it. But indifference, separateness, personified in some strange incredible almost tangible way.

Oh, now I knew what it was! It was the spirit of nature walking abroad this midsummer night!

I lay motionless, without even breathing, filled to bursting with a quiet ecstasy of awareness — waiting. Surely any minute now the spirit of nature would become visible. I strained my eyes. I waited — and waited...

I saw nothing.

Yet if suddenly Pan or a goat-legged satyr had emerged from behind a tree I should not have been surprised. I could have believed in anything on such a night.

Suddenly I understood. **This was how myths were born!** I knew it through feeling, not reason. Yet I had been taught that reason was the only respectable way to know anything.

All those fascinating Greek myths, for instance. They were not meaningless stories concocted by fanciful people. Such things sprang naturally from our own mysterious depths. For one fleeting moment tonight the impenetrable barrier had been lowered. I had been shown how the human race creates its myths and symbolical gods.

CHAPTER 6

FLOWERS

The young man to whom I was engaged arrived at our girls' college. He had come for the weekend from the nearby university. An unusual custom in those days. At Sunday noon dinner he laughed and braved the entire dining room of a thousand noisy chattering girls. He was the only male present.

"Let's escape to the farthest end of the campus," he said after dinner. "I want to take your picture and recover my equilibrium."

We strolled on and on out of sight of the vigilant faculty. We arrived at a wild wooded part of the campus where I had never been before. An overpowering fragrance rushed out to greet us. There standing alone against a clump of green trees stood an incredibly beautiful white tree. A small tree covered with a profusion of white blossoms. They hung down in long pendulant clusters like grapes.

"Oh, that's fine," he said. "That flowering locust will make an excellent background! I want to take your picture against it. Please stand over there, darling child. I don't know much about this darned Kodak. Borrowed it from my roommate. Wait till I get it adjusted properly."

He walked some feet away and busied himself with the camera. I stood motionless, speechless for a long moment, staring at this incredible sight. Never in my life had I beheld such an enchanting tree. Never had I inhaled such a — a provocative perfume. It was deeply disturbing.

Abruptly I turned my back on my companion. My face begged for a little privacy. I could not bear to reveal the poignant aching joy that surged through my whole body.

Why, this scent — it possessed a life, a meaning of its own! It was heavy, palpable, all but visible like some magic carpet in an Arabian Nights' story. Surely it possessed the power to bear anyone away to some fantastic land of eternal delight. But it was unbearably sweet.

"Flowers so sweet the sense faints
picturing them."[1]

So that was what Shelley meant!

Slowly I walked up to this tree, gently held a long cluster in my hand. Then suddenly I cupped the creamy white blossoms in both hands, pressed them passionately to my face, breathed in this intoxicating perfume deeper and deeper till all my senses swam in a sea of scent.

I held my breath. I must keep this marvelous fragrance locked inside me forever. It aroused my whole being to an intense listening state. I strained every nerve to catch that faint far-off message. What was it? This perfume of the locust seemed a faint reminder of some ideal plane of existence half-forgotten. For one brief ecstatic moment it seemed as if I recollected some previous state — idyllic and perfect. Could this fragrance be an elusive messenger from some indescribable other world from which I was now a temporary exile?

But I never had heard of Plato's theory of pre-existence. Yet as I lay awake that night I asked myself, does this extraordinary kind of experience mean that in our everyday life we are all being traitors to some deeper part of ourselves? Oh, would the great day of understanding never, never come?

"There's a great day a-coming!" the Negro spiritual promised. I wanted to believe it.

CHAPTER 7

CHILDREN

Can this kind of thing — unsought — unwelcome — be the origin of man's involuntary belief in a human soul?

On a balmy April day I witnessed a spectacle even I found incredible. I was a welfare director in an Alabama mining camp.

My contract stated that I was to conduct classes in the Community Club House in cooking and sewing for mothers and daughters of the miners. At the last minute a kindergarten was thrust upon me. I was appalled. I had no training. Not even nature's training. No younger brothers or sisters. I was not even maternal, alas.

Every morning twenty to thirty children assembled at the Club House. A handful came from official families, the majority from the miners' families. Many of them were ill-clothed, ill-bathed, ill-mannered, but all — yes, every child soon proved to be a daily delight.

From the very first hour some sort of idyllic spell seemed to hover over this group of children — why, I never knew. It was doubly puzzling because, when I visited these same children in their homes, they wounded me immeasurably by staring at me as if I were a total stranger. They shyly hid behind their mothers' dirty calico skirts.

I taught these children absolutely nothing. I was merely their leader. I was only twenty and a child myself in more ways than one, I fear.

Discipline? There was no such thing. Disorder? It didn't exist. Noise? It simply was a problem that never arose. Except when another adult entered the room.

On some mornings we sang our hearts out while I played the piano. On rainy days we sat before a huge open fire. I told them endless stories, my favorite little boy on my lap, the faces of half of them mimicking my every expression. Afterwards, with the greatest of ease we dramatized the nursery stories, without a stage, without rehearsal — but with infinite delight.

We strolled through the Autumn woods, gathered and named the species and varieties of colored leaves — and not one child ever strayed away. We took bird walks through the woods in the Spring, learned their colloquial names and nesting places. Not even the tough tobacco-chewing urchins of six threw their accustomed rocks.

Most delightful of all our projects was blowing soap bubbles. I always chose this pastime on a day when at least one child was absent. I wanted a pipe too.

One lovely warm April day we carried our bowls of soapy water and white clay pipes out to the great rolling lawn in front of the clubhouse. And that's when it happened.

The Community House was surrounded by beautifully landscaped grounds immaculately kept by our colored gardener. The Company claimed it was striving to transform the crude raw mining camps into model towns. It stubbornly maintained this was not philanthropy but merely good business. Healthy happy miners were less migratory and better workers.

Now the children commenced to blow their bubbles. I sank down on the grass to observe. One little boy sat staring at his string of bubbles flying from his pipe like a flock of geese in single formation. Another blew so hard his red face was round and distended like a bubble. A third child had no sooner achieved a beautiful bubble than he thrust his pudgy forefinger in it to deflate it.

A thin pale quiet girl labored intently each time to form one large perfect bubble. Then she would gaze after it fascinated as it rose higher and higher swaying and dancing in invisible currents of air like a dancer moving to inaudible music. It disappeared from sight long before it burst.

Some children tried too hard and failed. Some did not try hard enough and failed. Others blew with ease and invariably achieved good results. Some laughed with delight at the spectacle. Others were silent and pontifically solemn. A few of them sat idle and enjoyed observing others work or play. But none was indifferent. Each child's personality was revealed by his different method of blowing bubbles. What an illuminating lesson in psychology for an observer.

Brilliant sunshine flooded the whole scene. The sun laid a hot caress upon our bare heads and hands. The grass had been freshly mowed today and now gave off that delicious odor of watermelon for whose luscious red hearts I entertained such an inordinate passion. Along the fences tall rows of pink and white cosmos danced lazily in the wind like a merry but ill-trained ballet.

Vivid white puffs of clouds blown up from the Gulf of Mexico were piled like whipped cream against the deep heart-warming blue sky. That spring breeze had come from some enchanted land on the other side of the world. It whispered that just over the next red hill and far away lay the fulfillment of your favorite daydream.

And the air was filled with music unlike any other in the world. The lilt of happy children's voices and the poignant cadence of their laughter. It was enough to melt your heart even if it were as hard as a lump of bituminous coal.

Now the whole hillside was filled with dozens of dancing bubbles bobbing up and down and then bursting into nothingness. How odd — these little watercolored balloons did not shine with the usual white highlights of other rounded objects. But where they caught the sun every one was touched with all the opalescent colors of the rainbow. What law of physics explained this exception to the rule? I forgot. Some of the bubbles floated fitfully up on strange currents of wind, paused, wavered, glided down again like scores of small balloons released in a miniature festival to celebrate a miniature Spring.

I myself was now blowing bubbles lustily wishing this day would never, never end.

Without a word a little girl sank down beside me — a grubby, pudgy, coarse-faced child but one with a warm, eager, lovable personality. She leaned against me. The warmth of her body against mine, the gentle pressure of her head against my breast filled me with a strange kind of happiness I never had experienced before in my life. I put my arm around her in a vibrant content deeper than any I imagined existed. Tears of happiness blurred my sight. A sweet pain constricted my heart. I blew one slow enormous bubble from my pipe. The youngest boy, about three years old, ran laughing after it raising his helpless little hands to catch it — in vain.

The perfect moment of a perfect day! I sat there, my whole being supercharged with an unfamiliar impersonal kind of happiness. Suddenly these children running over the green earth appeared to be but **extensions** of the grass and flowers. Not separate but part of the same marvelous cosmic process. The budding of life itself. Spring personified.

All of a sudden such a flood of love for these small creatures issued from me, it seemed to flow over them like a gigantic stream of mother's milk. I felt my whole being dissolving utterly away. . .

Then suddenly I beheld the most phenomenal sight — or seemed to. I saw the very essence of childhood — the sweetness, the innocence emanating from them like a fragrance made visible. It rose from their bodies and floated above their heads. For one electrifying moment, these incredible objects appeared before my astonished eyes. Round but not closed at bottom and top. Nebulous in shape. Body outlines, envelopes, of faint iridescent colors. And barely discernible. But I would have sworn they exhaled a perfume all their own. Like the poignant fragrance that rises from the hair of a healthy child.

Then they vanished — like that! These lovely apparitions dissolved back into the sunshine almost in the same fleeting instant they formed.

Startled but too happy to be frightened, I accepted this phenomenon. On such an unnaturally happy day such an unnatural incident seemed only natural. Was it extra-sensory perception — or what?

Next I seemed to see something else even more fantastic! Not with my physical eyes this time but with my mind's eye. The true nature of these children not only now on earth but **before** birth! I saw their absolute purity of spirit. In a vague far-off place something like small white kernels standing upright — unsupported. Or were they small white flames inextinguishable and eternal, burning without source, destined to exist in the center of their beings?

Suddenly **through** these children today I recognized the intrinsic purity of **all** people. It was as if there existed deep in all of us something like a small white germinal seed of utter goodness. A kernel lying dormant, overlaid by an envelope of earthly flesh and worldly ways. Like that famous little piece of grain the scientists discovered recently. The one imprisoned in an Egyptian cornerstone, I think it was, over 2,000 years ago. When found it was still in its pristine fertile state — waiting — waiting — for the proper environment to grow again. Now I envisioned briefly the future life of man. A higher type of life on earth where man's potential purity was uncovered, allowed to flourish in another environment. One more propitious than the cold materialistic atmosphere of today.

Abruptly, this memory, or pretty fancy, or whatever, melted away. Nothing remained but ordinary flesh-and-blood children running about a very real earth pursuing very real soap bubbles. And a young girl sitting bemused on the grass bursting with joy and awe, fear and wonder.

I could scarcely wait to return home. It was nearly lunchtime so I dismissed the children early and ran back to the cottage. I must get there before the other welfare directors arrived.

Quickly I extracted my much-marked volume of Wordsworth concealed behind the other books in the communal living room. I carried it to the bathroom. This was the only spot of privacy in a house with four strong-minded Northern girls and one strong-minded cook. I perched myself on the only available seat. Then holding my breath, I read again Wordsworth's notes which preceded the poem. "Many times while going to school have I grasped at a wall or tree to recall myself from this abyss of idealism to the reality. . . . At that time I was afraid of such processes. I used to brood over stories of Enoch and Elijah and persuade myself that I should be translated to heaven."[1]

Well, I thought, I was not that far gone, thank goodness. Avidly I began to read the familiar poem with shining new understanding. The words expanded like light in my brain:

ODE

INTIMATIONS OF IMMORTALITY FROM
RECOLLECTIONS IN EARLY CHILDHOOD

"There was a time when meadow, grove, and stream,
  The earth, and every common sight,
    To me did seem
  Apparelled in celestial light."[2]

No, that did not explain it. I did not believe in celestial things, did I? I read on:

"The Soul that rises with us,...
  Cometh from afar:
  Not in entire forgetfulness,
  And not in utter nakedness,
 But trailing clouds of glory do we come
  From God, who is our home."³

So **that's** what "trailing clouds of glory" meant! So that's what I saw today!

I stared at the name of this poem incredulously. Why, the title of this poem — it was incorrect. This famous poem did not say anything about immortality. Not a word about life after death, only about life before birth.

I studied Wordsworth's prefatory notes again. "That dream-like vividness and splendor which invests objects of sight in childhood...I regarded as evidence of a prior state of existence...A pre-existent state has entered into the popular creeds of many nations; and among all persons acquainted with classic literature, is known as an ingredient in Platonic philosophy."⁴

"Pre-existence" — that word! I dashed out of the bathroom to look it up in the dictionary. Now I could hear the healthy athletic girls pounding up the front steps. Quickly I carried both books out to the sleeping porch where they could not see me.

I read the definition of "pre-existence" and my blood ran cold: "Existence of the soul before its union with the body." No, no, please! This was more than I could endure! Have mercy, please. I was drowning in abstract waters far over my head!

CHAPTER 8

POETRY

New York City was as glamorous as it was said to be — and more so. I had been living there for several years now — and loving every minute of it. When I left Alabama, I attended Columbia University primarily as an excuse to pacify my parents about my trip to the wicked city.

Externally my life appeared decorous and conventional enough. It revealed nothing of the turbulent drama surging underneath.

Every minute of the eighteen waking hours was filled to the brim with happy excitement. I loved my job. The pay was small, the hours long. I had chosen this type of work because I loved to look at books, to touch books, smell them, read them, discuss them with interested people. The only place offering this pleasure — with a salary — was a publishing house or a bookshop. Publishing houses looked like a remote heaven to me. So I worked in a bookshop. Several, in fact.

Of course my family, buried in the deep-South traditions of East Texas, considered working in any kind of **shop**, even one hallowed by books, *infra dig*. To protect their old-fashioned sensibilities, I refrained from telling them.

For the first time in my life I was doing exactly what I wanted to do. I was financially independent. I had an infinitesimal apartment, books, a piano (rented), and a place to write my own novel on Sundays and to think my thoughts in peace.

That was all I asked of life, to be allowed to be myself — however strange that creature might prove to be. I wanted to develop naturally like a straight young poplar tree reaching for the sun. I did not want to be shaped, pruned, pushed by home or church or school, by neighbors, friends, or even a husband. Freedom — that was all I asked of the world.

I did not want to marry anyone — not now, not yet. Not even the gayest and noblest, the wisest, and most quixotic man I ever had known. He was a British sculptor whose small exquisite bronzes were in the Metropolitan Museum.

Many interesting men, however, came into the bookshop to my delighted surprise. Soon my social life was a gay whirl. I saw nothing unusual in such a life. I was brought up in the dubious traditions of the Southern Belle. Every Southern girl reckoned herself a dismal failure unless men besieged her night and day.

It was exciting to go out almost every night. I reserved one evening a week, however, for myself. To reassemble the scattered fragments of my personality. Sometimes as I sat alone in the blessed solitude of my small apartment, I could feel myself expanding almost physically. Like those incredible Japanese flowers we had as children. You dropped a crinkled little bit of colored nothing into water. And lo and behold, it uncurled into a full-blown flower.

One Sunday night I sat writing unusually late. Finally I stopped, my back aching, my mind happy. In fact, I was happy about everything except that puzzling problem of traditional religion. It pursued me daily like a hound of heaven.

How could anyone worship anything which permitted evil in the world? Disease. Weakness. Ignorance. Ugliness. War. Poverty. Stupidity. Misery. Floods. Earthquakes. And worst of all, man's inhumanity to man. It was the old intellectual problem. Either God was not omnipotent or he was not benevolent — in which case, could he be a God? There was no answer.

Abruptly I picked up a small volume of verse lying ominously on my desk. It was a gift from the sculptor. We read aloud to each other constantly, discussing all the tabooed subjects. But I had carefully avoided reading this book. Now I opened it.

I began to read a poem. It was like plunging into a swift icy river. The shock of it was painful at first then warm and stimulating. I was swept along like a helpless swimmer in a dangerous current, being carried — where? I did not know.

> "I am that which began;
>   Out of me the years roll;
> Out of me God and man;
>   I am equal and whole;...
>
> Before ever land was,
>   Before ever the sea,
> Or soft hair of the grass,
>   Or fair limbs of the tree...
> ...I was...."[1]

Slower now, fearfully, I read each word separately. Every line dropped into my mind like a drop of priceless essential oil. Like the precious attar of roses

I often watched my chemist friend drop into alcohol when making perfume in his laboratory. Every phrase acted like a concentrated essence — spreading — transforming my whole mental content.

> "First life on my sources
>   First drifted and swam;
> Out of me are the forces
>   That save it or damn;
> Out of me man and woman, and wild-beast and bird;
>   Before God was, I am."[2]

That stopped me cold.

Finally I read on. The rhythm carried me along irresistibly. The meaning pierced like an icicle — alternately cold and burning.

> "Beside or above me
>   Nought is there to go;
> Love or unlove me,
>   Unknow me or know,
> I am that which unloves and loves; I am stricken, and
>   I am the blow."[3]

I stopped reading. Struck motionless, I sat there feeling as if I saw the whole world, and all that's in it being born, issuing from the vast womb of time. As if some mighty mouth of some mighty man had opened far up in the sky, as if all life were flowing from his lips till it was blown by the winds to the four corners of the earth.

Unity! Oneness out of many. Unity, ah, there was something you could comprehend, encompass. Diversity was too confusing, overwhelming. I had always thought of the separateness of everything. God up there, man down here. Then the earth and all the things upon it. Pantheism was an unknown word to me.

Suddenly it was as if I could see the great life force itself, like an incoming tide, flooding all the dry rivulets of the world. How glorious! So everything came from one source — the grass, the sea, everything we did, everything we failed to do, wars and peace, disease and death, joy and grief — good and evil — and even perhaps man's conception of God!

I thrust the book away. I could not read any more. It was too much. I closed it with reverent fingers, turned out the light and sat on at my desk in the darkness — overwhelmed — how, why, I did not know. I felt as we should feel in church but don't — happy, full of awe and sweetness as a Protestant imagines a nun must feel when she kneels at the altar touched by some holy mystery.

My body, mind, and spirit felt as if they had attained perfect harmony for this one glowing instant — with themselves, with the whole world, and everything beyond it. The equilibrium everywhere was apparent — in the stars, earth, mankind, and the great unknown. Everything swung gently in sweet balance — even evil appeared an essential counterpart to good — just how, I could not fathom. Somehow in a moment of direct intuitive insight, had a fleeting glimpse into the natural order of the cosmic scheme been granted me?

Suddenly it seemed as if the darkened room was filled with a great golden light. Not moonlight. Not sunlight. Nor man-made light. But a light unlike any I ever had seen before, living light. For in it I felt a presence, an invisible shining presence. A divine presence? But how could that be? I was no longer an orthodox believer.

But there was positively something there. Something vast, stupendous, cosmic. It was not a person yet it was alive — vibrant. A spiritual presence? An essence diffused in that golden light? Certainly a radiance filled the entire room.

Was it the spirit of the universe? I sat struck dumb with wonder. I was not frightened. I should have been. But in this phenomenal light I perceived a beneficence. A gentleness. It possessed a holiness as I never had felt holiness in anything before in my entire life. A sweet serenity. Even a suggestion of gentle humor as if it wished to reassure me, a mere mortal child bewildered and groping. Somehow it seemed as if it were rewarding me for something. What? I did not know.

I sat there — a quiet ecstasy of happiness suffusing me, a slow exaltation flooding me with ineffable joy.

How long this ecstatic state lasted I do not know. Abruptly this golden light vanished as inexplicably as it had come. I turned on the lamp again. Reverently I touched the title of that poem like a blind person, hoping my fingers could interpret what eyes and brain could not. Softly I uttered the title of the poem aloud, *Hertha*. Earth goddess.

Did Swinburne mean there might be some larger, more all-embracing conception of the creative power of the universe? An impersonal all-pervasive good, an inscrutable cosmical It? One common to all races and perhaps underlying all formal religions? One which might make all men akin if they could but enlarge their vision?

Was this the kind of ecstasy and insight the church was supposed to arouse in people? But a thousand times I had attended church in years past and nothing like this ever happened. A thousand times I had prayed, read the Bible. The nearest I ever came to such a sensation was when I sang their hymns. But the Christian hymns filled you with a cold sense of guilt and sin. This — this golden light flooded you with joy, with a warm sense of goodness — your own and everyone else's and especially the goodness of the life force itself.

To institutionalized religion, I had gone again and again an eager supplicant with open hands and open mind and empty heart asking it to fill me, feed me, lift me up. It had sent me empty-handed away every time. Who could live on meaningless dogma, devitalized phrases, dead cliches, and empty exhortations? But now a poem — one poem nourished me more than all the organized religions, churches and sermons. One little poem furnished what I had sought in the Bible, a living vital certainty of joyousness and goodness and serenity as the core of self, as the basis of life, as the secret of the universe. There was an unseen order in the universe. I did not understand it intellectually but I **felt** it, to the farthest reaches of my being.

I never had read William James' dictum that "the spirit of the universe is your own subconscious self."[4] I had no idea what was happening to me. But all the ratiocination of all the rationalists, all the scientific arguments of all the scientists on earth, even the laughter, the ridicule of those who never had been visited by such a glorious experience — none of these could alter my conviction one jot. I felt that I knew. What? Ah, I was not quite sure — yet. But it was something wonderful!

CHAPTER 9

THOUGHT

Can truth make us free?[1]

The unexpected answer to this unexpected question appeared the night the visiting British millionaire gave me that elaborate dinner party. He said it would stimulate my writing if I met other artists. It was staged at the apartment of two English friends of his, a writer and his wife.

Our hostess assured me there was no necessity to dress. A new long yellow evening gown hung eagerly in my closet. But I donned a short simple dinner dress. My escort, the sculptor, called for me in a sack suit.

When we arrived, our hostess and all the other women were decked out in cloth of gold evening gowns and half the crown jewels. The architect's face fell perceptibly as he stared at my short dress. Was that a gleam of triumph in my hostess' eyes?

At any other time I would have been embarrassed. Tonight it simply never occurred to me to explain or apologize. I was I, no matter what I wore, wasn't I? Whether a dress ended at a woman's knees or touched the floor, was decollete or semi-demi, seemed of marvelous unimportance. Was it because I was too absorbed in other problems — writing a book and struggling with man-made conventions, and the whole religious idea?

The sculptor of course was above embarrassment then and always. "Good form," however, was the god of the English. I had violated their sacred rites.

The dinner consisted of all the rarest delicacies money could buy, caviar, truffles, grouse, vintage champagne. I enjoyed these unaccustomed luxuries thoroughly. The conversation, however, was dominated by the hostess — not the artists. It was personal, trivial and dull. I longed to go home and write.

Later at my door I said goodnight to my sculptor friend and walked slowly into the apartment feeling extremely odd. For some unknown reason I did not turn on the light. I did not even undress. I sank to the edge of my hard narrow little bed and sat there in the dark — thinking — thinking — thinking. I sat there half the night. Or was it all night? I shall never know. For this was the night of the storm, the lightning and the glory! I was twenty-five.

For twenty-four years I had been a dutiful slave to all the conventions imposed on weak-willed women. But the whole last year marked a continuous revolt against all the conventions — good, bad, and indifferent.

Originally I had believed that when I freed myself from the restrictions of home and school and church I would be blissfully free. Free to act, think, speak, and dress exactly as I saw fit. I wasn't.

Then I was convinced that when I became self-supporting, that act would strike the last chains from my legs. It didn't.

Day after day, month after month, I felt the pressure of that invisible power — society. It dictated to me, to everyone — our opinions, our behavior, our manners — and especially the kind of clothes we should wear.

Why in heaven's name, I asked myself as I sat there in the dark tonight, must we all wear what "They" decree? No woman revels in pretty feminine clothes more than I, but fashion — that's tyranny.

Who is this who has the right to tell us we must wear dresses touching the ground after dark or be considered an inferior species? Who says we must wear dresses above our knees in the daytime? There never was a beautiful knee-cap in the world — least of all mine. What if I prefer long dresses in the day-time? Then I'd be considered queer — eccentric. Does that make sense?

Who in God's name are these people who decide my fate, every woman's fate, so arbitrarily? By what law must all women this year wear hats jammed down to their eyebrows, next year large hats, and the year after small hats perched on the back of their heads to fly off in every breeze? You never see these mysterious arbiters of our destinies. Whence do they derive their power? Do we women give it to them? Are we even consulted? Why do we wear short hair if we prefer long, and long nails when we prefer short? Why don't we all have the right to walk down Fifth Avenue barefoot if we wish? Or even naked? We are born naked, aren't we?

Well, we have the right. But we should be laughed at, even arrested merely for being different from the majority.

Oh, yes, you must never be different from your fellows. That is the supreme crime. Conform, conform, submit, imitate, follow, obey blindly, stupidly.

I rose and paced the floor in extreme agitation. Shouldn't innate kindness be our guide to good manners? Not artificial rules of etiquette.

And ideas — must we submit like sheep to constantly changing fashions in opinions too?

Recently I had followed first Mencken, then Sinclair Lewis, then Renan and next Romain Rolland and other literary explorers in that dark and dangerous land of thought. For the last five years I had felt like an amateur adventurer in darkest Africa — lost in the vast jungle of other people's ideas. Trails led off in all directions. But which one would carry me to the highest mountain in the world where the absolute truth was set like a rare jewel?

I sank to the edge of the bed again. I clasped my hands together in anguish, murmuring: I feel, I think, but I do not know. My ignorance is too painful. I must know that I know. All my life I have felt like a little green plant growing under the hard black earth, pushing my obstinate young head against the ground. Like those tightly curled fern leaves you see in the woods in early spring. Someday surely I will burst through into the light of certitude. But when? **When?** Can thought — if intense enough, if prolonged enough — open the gates of truth to us?

Suddenly it felt as if everything inside my body was being shaken by a mighty earthquake. My physical surroundings faded away. But I did not become unconscious. Rather all my faculties felt heightened tremendously, almost superconscious. A vibrant awareness, a glowing intensity became so great it surpassed anything that seemed possible to a mere human body. It was utterly indescribable.

Elation mounted steadily. Now I seemed to see before me a great mountain. It was not an external sight. It obviously was an outward projection of my feelings and thoughts. But the sensations were so vivid it all felt exactly like an actual physical experience.

Now I was climbing this formidable mountain. The air grew rarer and rarer. I felt light-headed, intoxicated by such pure air. Fear assailed me yet I continued to climb up and up against my own volition. I was no longer my own master. Some mighty force propelled me.

Finally I reached the top of the highest peak in the world — a bald bare rock. I lay there exhausted panting for breath. A premonition of some awful wonder about to burst upon me made my body tremble uncontrollably. I looked up at the dark menacing sky.

Abruptly two black storm clouds rolled back like mighty curtains in the sky. Between them burst unearthly light. A light of overpowering brilliance. It all but blinded me. Every atom of my being vibrated with a warm golden exultation delicious beyond endurance. Oh, surely I was not in danger, like the prophet Elijah in the Bible, of being translated and ascending straight to some unknown heaven?

No, no, please, I begged, deliver me from such unbearable ecstasy. The splendor, the grandeur of this transcendent light — surely no mortal can look upon such a sight and live!

If I looked again I should be blinded. I should die! But look I must!

Suddenly for one awful moment there appeared that which is intolerable to human eyes. I gazed into the glowing core of the cosmos, "pierced the great enigma." Something in me seemed to communicate directly with the great life force...

Did I faint from sheer bliss?...

Eons of time passed...

Finally new ebullient life began to stir in my forgotten limbs. Suddenly the constrictions of society dropped away like an outworn cloak. Exultant, I leapt to my feet on the mountain top. The iron edicts of convention fell away like chains from my legs.

I was naked, naked on the mountain top with nothing to cover me but my own confidence. I flung my arms to heaven laughing with unholy glee. I shouted exultantly. New knowledge poured into my poor bursting little brain. In a flash I perceived truths which logic and reason had long sought in vain.

Laws? What are they but a few stupid words written on paper by a few men as stupid and ignorant as I.

Ideas! What are they but the opinions of people no wiser than you and me!

Conventions! What are they but imitations of others by people too weak to stand alone.

Clothes? Styles? Fashion? They are man-made. Why be their slave! Nature's man, isn't he born naked?

Fine **houses?** A piece of stone to crumble in a few years!

Jewels! Nothing but minerals like coal dug out of the earth, strung around women's necks, called valuable by people, valueless surely in the great scheme of the universe.

God? Why, he is not a great omnipotent man up there in the sky spying on your every act like a vindictive detective. He is this — this blinding light! This dazzling source of truth...

And the truth shall make you free.

I am free, at last, free of the whole world! Free of what other people think and say, free of their opinions of me, of everything! I am my own master henceforth.

From this moment I shall be a law unto myself. I shall make my own laws, my own conventions, do my own thinking!

For now I know! And I know that I know. I have felt, I have thought, but now I **know!** I have discovered Truth! For this mental freedom, this certitude, I have waited and prayed and strained my being. For this I have lived and suffered and doubted. Ourself! Ah, that is the secret of life. I see it now. **Within ourselves we must look for all things.** For truth, freedom, goodness, guidance, even God — not to men, society, laws, or books. Our own deepest purest thoughts and feelings are as near the truth as any man's. For in some mysterious place within us all, nature has inexplicably buried her greatest treasures.

Gradually that glorious afflatus ebbed away. Once more the bed, the room, became realities.

Could this be the kind of light, the kind of ecstasy, the men who wrote the Bible felt? Good God Almighty, that was blasphemy even to an agnostic! That way lay madness.

Without warning or reason I felt a compulsion to go to the bookcase. Was it my unconscious mind? At twenty-five I never had heard this term used psychologically. Rising, I turned on the light. Without the slightest hesitation my hand extracted a green and gold book purchased many months before and never opened.

I disliked this book very much. It has been thrust down the unwilling throats of most American children in High School. Its exhortatory tone was too similar to that of a minister. It had gone out of intellectual fashion. But Emerson was a classic therefore I purchased it and added it to my small growing library. I was waiting for the great day when I should grow up to it mentally.

Now I opened it. Certain passages leapt out at me. I could not believe those astounding words.

"As far as we can recall these ecstasies, we carry away in the ineffaceable memory the result, and all men and all ages confirm it. It is called truth!"[2]

"To believe your own thought, to believe that what is true in your private heart is true for all men — that is genius."[3]

"All our progress is an unfolding, like the vegetable bud. You have first an instinct, then an opinion, then a knowledge, as the plant has root, bud and fruit. Trust the instinct...it shall ripen into truth."[4]

"And truly it demands something godlike in him who has cast off the common motives of humanity and has ventured to trust himself for a taskmaster...Every man is an inlet...What Plato has thought, he may think: what a saint has felt, he may feel."[5]

"The highest merit we ascribed to Moses, Plato, and Milton is that they set at naught books and traditions and spoke not what men, but what *they* thought. A man should learn to detect that gleam of light which flashes from within, more than the luster of the firmament... Yet he dismisses without notice his thought, because it is his. In every work of genius we recognize our own rejected thoughts."[6]

"All goes to show that the soul of man is not an organ...is not a faculty...but a light."[7]

"We distinguish the announcements of the soul, by the term *Revelation*. These are always attended by the emotions of the sublime. For this communication is an influx of the Divine mind into our mind."[8]

CHAPTER 10

THE CITY

I was going to die apparently. The doctors announced they were unable to do any more for me. A major operation and a mysterious illness had exiled me from my beloved city of New York. Three wasted interminable years had dragged by in a small town in Texas. Here I had been so happy as a girl but now felt like an alien.

One day I lay on the bed with closed eyes dreaming of the city of cities. A kitten sat on my chest purring blissfully. I was not well enough to read or write or talk or even walk more than a block. My cat and my thoughts were my only entertainment.

My father and mother had been the epitome of patience and kindness. After a separation of seven years our lives ran like parallel rivers never merging.

My grandmother and her provincial friends, however, informed me daily of my crimes: "You love the city more than your own home town," they said. "You love all the wild free life of that wicked New York better than the wholesome normal life of the provinces. You love the theater and opera more than going to church, other books more than the Bible, the arts more than God."

"We could not bear to live in the city," the grandmothers continued. "It has no birds or flowers, no sunshine or fresh air. There are no friendly neighbors, no good fresh food, nor quiet. And worst of all, no trees."

I was too weak to argue. But why, I wondered, did I, a small-town girl born in a provincial town in Texas, 2,000 miles from New York, surrounded by love and comfort, by flourishing cotton fields, friendly (underprivileged) Negroes, and crumbling aristocratic tradition — why did I love the city so passionately?

As I lay there stroking my imperturbable cat today, a silent dialogue shaped itself between the eternal provincials and the converts to the city:

There are no lovely **birds** in the city, protest the grandmothers.

But **ideas**, we explain, ideas flock to the city like millions of brilliant migratory birds. The city is the only place new species can find a safe breeding ground.

No **flowers**, they say, can bloom in all that carbon monoxide.

But **you** bloom, we insist. Your personality blossoms out in the city of stone. Your mind (if you have one) your wit (if you possess any) your charm and talent are nourished daily by warm response.

But there's no **sunshine** in those dark narrow streets.

But there's the light of **freedom**. Have you never felt freedom light up your way like the dazzling noonday sun?

No friendly **neighbors** there. It must be lonely.

Yes, thank God, we admit. **Privacy**, that rarest of all luxuries, exists only in the city. Only in the sweet solitude among strangers can you build your own system of values with no one to observe your first fumbling failures. Of course you may die alone and no neighbor will care. But who ever thinks of death in the city of eternal youth?

There's no fresh **air**, the small town advocates continue.

But the air of **success!** we exclaim. Have you never breathed that heady air of success that pervades the city of cities? It's intoxicating!

The city lacks fresh **food**, they complain. It's too far from good wholesome farms.

But there's the feast of the **arts**, we say. You can partake of the best in America! The best in the world is imported from every country. Paintings, books, plays, music. And the conversation — it is the champagne of the district, a rare vintage grown only in the city, impossible to transport. It causes wit to sparkle, ideas to bubble up, laughter to effervesce.

But there is no **quiet** in the city, the provincials insist.

True, we agree. But who cares about noise when you can see such wondrous **sights?** You can stand at the window of any tall building and see giant ships from all over the world lying at your feet in the mighty Hudson. And the deep wistful wail of the fog horns wakens you at night and you are glad. It is the world knocking at your door.

And the **shops**, we continue, you can walk along Fifth Avenue and see all the greatest treasures of the earth displayed in the luxurious Fifties.

And **people** from all over the globe make a colorful parade on the street every day. New York is the city of beautiful women. Old women slim and vivacious looking like girls — all but their faces. Beautiful young women gowned and groomed till they're minor works of art. Handsome healthy men radiating success — sophisticated, amusing, well bred, and well educated.

Worst of all, the small town spokesmen finally say, there are no **trees**. We could not live without God's green trees.

But, we contend, what of the man-made forest of stone and steel, the magical **skyscrapers?** That tall incredible species which burst into bloom every night with a million flowers of yellow light? And by day wears the very clouds upon their lofty heads like careless veils?

What of that eighth wonder of the world which people come half way across the earth to see? The famous Manhattan sky line. It greets you across the Bay when you return on a majestic ship from Europe or a humble little ferry boat from Staten Island.

There it stands — a city of dreams-come-true, rising incredibly from the blue sea, the tall spires floating in a mist of mauve and distance and enchantment. Palaces more fabulous than fairy tales, fit only for the most noble princes and princesses. An island of stone castles, grey and white and pink, all bathed by day in poignant blue haze. By night they rise up black as onyx, silhouetted against the golden glow of the city sky decked with a million twinkling yellow diamonds of light.

No poet ever lived who could describe the magical mystical city of night.

My grandmother did not hear my paean in praise of the city. But even I had not known the city could perform miracles.

If I must die, I decided today, at least I might have the solace of dying in the city I loved. So I left the land of my birth and went home again — to my adopted city, the only place where I ever had felt completely at home in my adult life.

When the boat from Galveston docked in the North River, one of my faithful friends met me. He drove me to the hotel but I pleaded for immediate rest. Instead I wanted to walk slowly down Fifth Avenue from Fifty-ninth Street — alone. My knees were weak, my body unutterably weary. Slowly I crossed over to the East side of Fifth and strolled nostalgically down the Avenue. Nibbling at candy and crackers to maintain my energy, I smiled. I had been taught as a child that it was ill-mannered to eat on the street. At every block I was obliged to stop and rest while gazing in some shop window. Gradually I began to taste the heady flavor of the great city once more.

Through the very soles of my feet I felt it — the throb of the city, its rhythmic pulsing beat. The vitality of the city, why, it was sending new blood coursing through my pallid veins. Merely to walk down Fifth Avenue was to breathe faster, think faster. Here you drank from the mainstream of life, not the backwaters.

The rushing river of pedestrians carried me along effortlessly. The tall cliffs rising on each side of this stone canyon carried my eyes, my spirit, upwards, always upward.

But should I not be sensible, hail a taxi, and return to the hotel? But this might be the last time I ever walked down this beloved street.

Slowly I continued to stroll down Fifth Avenue. Then suddenly I saw It for the first time in my life. Abruptly I stopped, struck motionless at the corner of Forty-sixth. There a dozen blocks to the south, springing out of the ground like some fabulous blue flower reaching for the sky, was that celebrated new skyscraper at Thirty-fourth Street. Today it literally thrust its head up into the skies. The top was veiled behind moving white clouds as I had dreamed all New York skyscrapers would be when I was a thin green girl dreaming daydreams in that Alabama mining camp instead of rehabilitating the poor miners.

Today the whole east side of Fifth Avenue was flooded with sunshine. That faraway tower, however, was wrapped in soft blue mists and sweet melancholy. It stood there soaring high above all the lesser skyscrapers, above the city, above the world. It stood completely alone against all the illimitable space of infinity, triumphant, proud and unconquerable. The tallest building in the world, symbol of the greatest city in the world. The tower of towers.

I stood there staring at it like any provincial. Is it only the provincials, I wondered, who feel the mighty impact of the city? Surely thousands of others must feel as I do when they gaze at this fabulous tower. Our eyes cling to it because we know we are safe at last. Like sailors home from the sea, like soldiers home from the war, we have come home. This great grey shaft marks the end of a journey. The answer to questions too deep to voice. A vast exclamation point marking the end of our sentence of death. The pivot about which our new lives can revolve.

Is it not the symbol of stability? Permanence embodied in stone? A monument to strength, delicacy and beauty? A finger pointing to infinity? That miracle in stone — the Empire State tower.

As I stood there old fears, old illness, weakness, bitterness, and rebellion were being washed away. My failing spirit and feeble limbs stirred with new life. Like medieval man exalted by the great Gothic cathedral spire, I felt the skyscraper was the modern symbol of all that was lofty in this life — if not in the next.

Automatically I moved on with the surging tide of pedestrians but stopped finally at the corner of Forty-fifth. Like a fragile steel magnet this blue spire surely drew to itself all the scattered fragments of the city's secret aspirations.

Did it not make us also long to reach for the sky, thrust our heads into the clouds, rise soaring above our petty material surroundings, above illness, and evil? Lend us energy to stand proudly alone, to become a tower of delicate strength to sustain others?

It filled this provincial with yearning to build a tower not of stone but of words, to create a book that might be a source of strength, truth, affirmations.

Suddenly a fountain of joy at merely being alive rushed through me. A strange new strength flooded all my limbs. Now I knew I would never die! I should be well and happy and see my dearest dream fulfilled.

CHAPTER 11

WRITING

My book was accepted. It was the second I had written, the first to be published. I had been working on it for four years at night.

The editor's magic letter constituted the high moment for which I'd waited a lifetime. Later when I held my first book in my hand, I felt the deep elemental happiness of a mother holding her newborn child. Then came interviews by the press, pictures in the papers, publisher's luncheon with ten men (I was the only woman present — a perfect arrangement), dancing in the most glamorous night club in New York with the tall handsome publicity director. It was delightful.

In bookshops I observed clerks swallow their excitement as I had done at the sudden appearance of Bertrand Russell, Sinclair Lewis, Dorothy Thompson and other literary celebrities. It was touching. The bookshop where I once had worked filled its entire window with my books. It was gratifying.

Letters of praise arrived from James Branch Cabell saying, "your book is indubitably a masterpiece"; from Burton Rascoe saying, "it is original, daring and profound"; from Aldous Huxley, "it is an extraordinary achievement" and from Carl Van Doren, "it is a beautiful book — one of my favorites." I was grateful for their encomiums, rather tepid to my lurid daydreams of impossible fame and fortune. All these pleasures of having a first book published were deeply gratifying. But they did not compare with the incredible excitement of writing it.

Every night, every Sunday and holiday, I wrote. Every weekday I managed a bookshop. Gladly I forsook all social life. All except lunch with women friends and dinner with men friends, provided they brought me home by eight o'clock.

My novel related how a young girl was lost in the desert of doubt, attacked by outlawed questions, climbed the Mountains of Casuistry, fell victim to the tropical fever known as love, and searched all over the world for that highest mountain on earth, known to man as Certitude.

For two whole years I wrote. Sometimes I felt like a mother with child. I carried the book with me wherever I went — inside me — like a great weight, a welcome weight. I fed it, gave it all my thought, time and love — gladly. I was never lonely.

Often I glanced down at my slender body amazed. I expected to see a large protuberance in front like a nine-months child, so physical was the creative process.

Like a prospective mother, I preserved my health for **"its"** sake, relinquished late hours and parties, forsook cocktails so my head would be clear, methodically took the exercise I loathed to help "it," ate sparingly so my brain would function clearly, even avoided becoming irritated with irritating people.

On other days I felt not like a mother at all but like a lover with a fickle mistress. I fell in love with the creative process.

I did not care whether I ever talked to any one else or not. I did not care whether I ate or what or when. I did not care whether I slept, or exercised, or even bathed. For the first time I understood why those astonishing Greeks personified the creative faculty as beautiful young women to be wooed — the nine Muses.

Usually words flowed without effort. Sometimes, however, ideas refused to appear. In desperation I paced the floor, clutched my hair, pounded my silly forehead with my fists — furious — frustrated. Nothing would come when forced and if it did, it was no damned good — dry — lifeless — pedestrian — dull.

I begged, I pleaded. The perverse lady remained absent.

Finally in disgust, I would say to hell with you. I'd lie down on the couch, turn my back on the manuscript scattered all over the desk and floor. I'd read a better book by a better man. Famous allegories — *Pilgrim's Progress, Erewhon, Jurgen, Candide*.

The instant I ceased thinking about my work that sly creature would reappear. She would cajole, tease, leave me no peace till I listened to her. I would leap up and begin typing again like a mad thing. Oh, it was wonderfully exhilarating!

I laughed to see ideas intruding at the wrong time and place. In bed in the middle of the night, as I walked along the street, as I sat at the lunch table, or in the bathroom. Colorful sentences, even phrases, were like bright tropical birds. If I failed to catch them by the tail instantly as they flew by, they would vanish never to return. I scribbled illegible notes on menus, on the back of old envelopes, match holders, or toilet paper. I could not bring myself to carry a notebook. It seemed so ostentatious. I was not a professional writer — yet!

Other strange new sensations crept unbidden onto the scene. Especially on Sunday afternoons. I wrote all the long heavenly day on Sundays. In the late afternoon I fell exhausted on my bed, my back aching, my shoulders cramped, my fingers tingling and sore from pounding the typewriter keys for hours, the callous throbbing on my middle finger from the pencil I used when correcting typescript, my brain whirling like a merry-go-round, my blood rushing through my body like a torrent in Spring flood.

I lay there weary but happy, trying to rest, still full of the fervor of creation. All the atoms of my being danced like those thousand golden dust moats I could see moving in a ray of sunlight that streamed in through my south window. Every pore of my skin was like a little hungry mouth longing to be kissed. The very blood in my veins ran hot and sweet like thick fruit liqueur — intoxicating me. It was painful — sweet — wonderful — strange.

It interfered with my work. I left my apartment on Twelfth Street, rushed down to Washington Square and walked around and around the Park until the disturbance spent itself.

Three years passed. Years of steady nightly writing. The book was half-finished and half accepted by a publisher. I borrowed money from the richest person I knew, resigned my position in the bookshop, and wrote all day. Exultation became my daily companion.

Reluctant to stop long enough to eat lunch, I usually tossed a can of chili con carne or tamales in a pan of hot water. Later I ate it with my left hand while my right corrected the typescript.

Then I would sit back and savor the pleasure which comes to all writers:

Words, you discover — they are neglected diamonds. Wash them in your own warm emotion and they sparkle like scintillating jewels.

Phrases lure you like dangerous sirens. Sometimes you become so enamored of the beauty of their music, you don't know what they're saying — or care.

Sentences — at times they swing through the air with the greatest of ease like trapeze performers, headed for certain disaster, landing safely back at their starting point with a skill which takes even your breath away.

Paragraphs stand before you like large blocks of beautifully polished marble. Adroitly you transpose them. Occasionally the most beautiful block of all fits nowhere. You weep to discard it.

Humor sometimes peeps unbidden from behind your most serious ideas, running like a mischievous imp between your soberest lines.

Emotion — joy or anger, occasionally rush unexpectedly through the pages like a turbulent river carrying the ideas and the reader (you hope) effortlessly along with it.

Like a proud craftsman you finally stand back and admire the strong framework supporting the whole architectural structure, invisible to the casual layman's eye.

And then you know, no man has lived until he has created something beautiful.

One night in the fourth year, I had been writing for hours. Never had the words flowed with such shining swiftness. I forgot where I was. I forgot time and place, whether I had eaten or not, whether it was night or day, Sunday or Monday, Fall or Spring. I forgot myself utterly and completely. I ceased to exist as a person, as a personality. I was scarcely aware of my body. I was merely an instrument.

Suddenly it seemed as if a broad shining river of dazzling light loosed itself from the sky. It flowed from far away up there in space right down into my own poor bursting little brain. I could feel the story flow from the river of light, through my arm, out the end of my pencil, onto the page.

It rushed on and on in a swift bright stream. I did nothing. I seemed to be merely an instrument of some higher power speaking through me, an empty vessel through which this glory elected to flow.

I trembled with fear and awe.

Everything was illuminated with a great white light whose source was invisible. Ecstasy descended out of the luminous nowhere agitating me with ineffable sensations. Some tremulous something within me vibrated like a throbbing golden force.

My mind felt as pure and cold as a crystal spring bubbling up from some hidden depths. All potentialities within me felt now fulfilled, every ounce of good, every atom of truth, freed for constructive use. This merciless light searched down to the rock most bottom of my best self, releasing it. All my vague yearning to serve my fellowman here found outlet. Would I not speak the vital life-saving truths, free myself and others from stultifying half-truths?

Breathless, I wrote on and on at white heat — suspended in a world of utmost perfection — no fear, no evil, no doubts. A world where I loved everything and everybody, where all was harmony and beauty — without beginning and without end. I felt purified, regenerated, filled with compassion for the whole human race. Filled with infinite power.

Then I knew that every serious artist feels like a god creating a new world — bringing order out of chaos.

In the beginning the writer's world of words was without form and void. So he created man in his own image — male and female created he them. He formed man from the dust of mere words and breathed into his nostrils the breath of life.

He looked forth at everything he had made, and, behold, it was good. And he rested from all the work which he had made.

Surely the creative impulse and the religious urge could not derive from the same source within us? What did it all mean?

CHAPTER 12

SEA AND SAND

Recently I had fallen ecstatically in love, married, quarreled and now had run away to my old comforter — the sea.

On Saturday morning my husband arrived at the small seaside hotel. His white face, his trembling hands smote me with contrition. My emotions rioted in every direction at once filling me with remorse — anger — love — relief — joy — and wounded pride.

After a dismal week of rain, the weather celebrated our deliriously happy reunion with a perfect seaside day. Hot penetrating sun. Dry clean air. A small cool breeze. We left the inn and walked toward the beach, our bathing suits tucked under our arms. A bride and groom never can recapture that first fine careless rapture of the wedding day, I had assumed. I was wrong.

"Your face is radiant," my husband whispered.

And so was his. The storms of a dozen violent emotions apparently had swept us clean. Never had I felt so vibrantly alive in my life. Mind, heart, and flesh tuned to concert pitch, ready instruments to all the glorious symphonies of life.

We strolled along the water's edge, beyond the bathers.

It was one of those rare Long Island days. The sun was satisfying hot, yet a low white mist lay along the sand — a diaphanous curtain to our right and left screening us from other eyes.

My husband climbed to the top of the embankment, glanced in all directions, ran down again, and flung his clothes to the ground with laughing disdain. Then with a wild shout of glee he ran naked into the sea.

Quickly I dropped my clothes to the ground, with every layer discarding layers of artificial civilization. It was the first time in my life I had gone swimming without a suit. With a happy shout I too ran into the sea. Today, **he** was there to save me so I could abandon myself to the waves as I never dared before.

I commenced to swim as fast and furiously as my untrained arms could carry me. Not bravely out to sea, but cautiously in the troughs between the waves. The mighty breakers charging toward me like a thundering herd of wild sea horses — their white manes blowing in the wind, their fierceness spent however before they reached me.

Panting for breath I was forced to stop swimming. But the sea never stops. Abruptly it buoyed me up in its strong arms like a gentle cruel lover. I lay floating idly, half-submerged. The waves lifted me on a gentle swell, my spirit lifted too on a mysterious wave of joy. What was I but a helpless bit of seaweed for the sea to do with as it pleased, its plaything — a piece of flotsam or was it jetsam — without will of my own?

Floating in my own delicious sensations, I feared, I hoped, I was becoming part of the green and white water, moving with it like white foam, being swept far out into the deepest ocean never to return. That would be the final joy. I should be going home again...

The sea — the strong cruel beautiful sea — was the male principle of the universe, its embrace rivaling all others, its kiss the kiss of death. Or of life everlasting?

I lay submerged in the elements, in timeless time, in a sweet diffusion of content, an unreasoned sense of permanent security, a cosmic embrace — all striving suddenly ended — all doubts finally dispelled...

"Come out of the water before you get too cold!" my husband shouted.

Blindly, in a daze, I followed him back to the shore. The wind and sun dried our skins with incredible rapidity.

He flung up his arms and shouted at the sky. "God damn it, I never expect to be this happy again so long as I live! Nothing so wonderful as this could happen but once in any two people's lives." Then he turned to me. "Now I'm going to build you the biggest bonfire that ever was made in the whole cockeyed world."

He ran off to gather driftwood, naked as Adam and twice as happy. My eyes followed him, my heart nearly bursting. I too felt as innocent, as pure as Eve in the beginning of the world.

All afternoon we played. We dashed in and out of the water repeatedly, each time better than the last. We didn't get cold, we didn't get hot, we didn't get tired. It was perfect, the weather was perfect, the sea, the sand was perfect. Life was perfect. Love and even marriage were going to be perfect henceforth, weren't they?

I went into the water one last time. The wind had shifted, it flung spray into my face. I licked my wet lips. How salty it tasted, how good!

This time I ventured out farther to the high roaring wall of green surf, stood directly under the giant breakers, let the water pour down dangerously on top of my head and shoulders like a small Niagara. The undertow tugged strongly at my legs. But my feet desperately searching for the bottom — they could not touch anything! A streak of cold terror ran through me exhilarating me all the more.

Now I noticed moving toward me one of those slow ominous tidal waves. I knew it was the most dangerous type. Hypnotized, I stared at it, treading water. It knocked me over, filling my eyes and nose and mouth with water, blinding, choking me. Now my head felt a thousand feet under black, strangling, suffocating water. Never would I reach the surface again.

Surely this was the drowning, the death I had feared a hundred times. But today I did not care too much. To die at this supreme moment of love and reconciliation, bathed in nature's wonder, might even be a pleasure. Despite all my high falutin ideas, now the animal instinct for survival asserted itself. I fought and scrambled, spluttered and coughed in a desperate effort to save myself. Suddenly in laughing disgust the sea flung me back with violent force onto the rough pebbles as if I were an inanimate piece of useless driftwood.

Dazed, I picked myself up, blood running from my cut knees and elbows. I loved it.

Exhausted I sank to the warm dry sand, lay stretched full length, panting, the dry pain in my chest burning with every indrawn breath. Never before in my entire life had I lain naked on the good warm earth. Women are not free as men are. Now I felt comforted like a child come home to its mother. It was good, good, all through my flesh, into the very marrow of my bones it felt good! Was not the earth the female principle of the universe, reminder of forgotten fundamentals?

Gradually every ounce of weariness, every atom of bitterness, every sorrow old or new slipped quietly into the sand like water. Suddenly I knew that waves and wind and sun can leave us immaculate as a seashell if we but lie still and allow them their wonders to perform.

I lay there — my blood laughing in my veins, my flesh tingling. I felt vibrant, triumphant, ready to attack any obstacle. Fatigue — what was that? Rest — who wanted to rest? Buoyant, I leapt to my feet and ran along the shore. The hot burning sand was good under my cold bare feet. Soft, resilient, alive. Not hard and unresponsive like the wooden floors of our houses, not cold and dead like the cement walks of our cities. To touch the earth — wasn't it to touch stability, permanence, the very source of life itself?

I ran along the firm edge of the sand laughing and dancing, my wet hair streaming out behind me. The sun pressed its fertile kiss emphatically on top of my head. How delicious to feel the cool breeze on my bare wet skin, the hot sun kissing me all over as I never had been kissed before. It was strange and wonderful.

As I danced, I sang at the top of my lungs (badly, I can scarcely carry a tune, always a half note off).

Swinging my arms high, improvising the steps as I went, I danced faster and faster. On and on I went, my muscles moving with delicious oiled smoothness, my blood surging warmly beneath my skin. They washed away every impurity of thought, and feeling, flooding me with the internal freshness of an innocent child in the morning of the world.

Gradually the rhythmic motion of my own muscles intoxicated me with the wild strange joy of primitive dancers in their religious rituals. Faster and faster I danced. Self-hypnotized, I never wanted to stop. The brief occasional touch of my feet to the earth only accented the beat of the music. Surely I was dancing in rhythm with the moving waves, the recurrent sun, the seasonal earth, and the unknown universe — in harmony with all natural things.

Soon the tug of the earth became too strong, drawing me magnetically toward it. Were the sand and sea, the wind and wave claiming their own again? Were my body and spirit threatening to return to the elements of which in some blissful state they once had been a part?

Quickly I commenced to leap through the air higher and higher, loving the wind through my hair. I leapt higher than high till I seemed to sever all connection with the earth forever, till I felt light as a bird on the wing, knowing an unearthly sense of freedom. Like a seagull sailing effortlessly on a down current wind. Like a spray blown up from the crest of a wave. It was sheer delight.

Then suddenly everything changed.

I know nothing of levitation but I am sure I did **not** remain suspended in mid-air yet I **felt** as if I did. For abruptly all sense of bodily motion ceased, all physical sensation, all conscious contact with the sand, for the earth itself no longer existed. Nor did the sky or sun or sea nor love nor giving in marriage nor even husbands.

I was alone in the universe with the universe.

I felt disembodied. Then even my inmost individuality itself seemed to be crumbling away like a child's castle of sand caught in the incoming tide.

A fathomless blackness was drawing me into itself as mysteriously as a magnet. Toward what? Dissolution? Disintegration? Was it a foretaste of death?

Then came a fearful bliss, an indescribable joy. A warm golden expansiveness within, a warm vibrance. I felt as if I had existed from the beginning of creation. I would continue to exist in this present blissful state forever. Was it intimations of immortality?

Now I felt myself melting, merging, with some great golden diffuseness, suspended in some vast luminous void. Time stood still...

Gradually consciousness of my physical surroundings returned. I stumbled blindly across the beach to the bonfire my husband had built. Panting violently I sank to a drift log, frightened, happy, puzzled. I dared not mention this mysterious experience to any living soul, especially a man. It might make him love a woman less.

But could this be what the Buddhist meant by Nirvana?[1] Or the dervishes by their whirling dances which induced religious feelings?[2] I knew less than nothing about any Oriental religions except from occasional references to them in my reading.[3] [4]

Besides, I wanted no part of mysticism, thank you, if that was what it really was. Everyday life was quite exciting enough for me now that I had a fine husband and home, and had tasted the depths of love, the high ecstasy of passion (which was like a religious experience itself sometimes) and the sweet enrichment of marriage.

CHAPTER 13

WINTER

It was eight o'clock one February night. I was waiting for my husband to come home for dinner.

I lighted the candles, arranged the flowers for the tenth time, straightened the silver again, returned to the kitchen, lighted the broiler, and admired the thick beautiful steak once more — and waited. If he was dining at his mother's again, why didn't he phone and tell me as he usually did?

After he had brought his runaway bride back home from the seashore last August, such happiness had surged through our beloved little apartment, it was unbearably sweet — for two weeks. Then it had all started again — the mystery — the days of silence — the white suffering face. Some mysterious grief was consuming him like a cancer. He refused to discuss it.

Nevertheless we both had tried every measure our bewildered brains could devise to save our beautiful marriage from being wrecked. We had descended from the peak of ecstasy. Now we were lost in some frightening strange country, visible to each other but unable to communicate.

Tonight I paced slowly from room to room. Hope and joy lay heavy as an unborn child dead within me. I glanced listlessly out the north window to note the progress of the winter storm.

But wait — what an astounding spectacle! The whole white world had gone mad. Tonight the snowflakes were waging the fierce battle against each other. Like avenging furies they flew first this way, then in the opposite direction. Suddenly they wheeled, plunged downward like long phalanxes of slanting white spears. Now they swirled upward in angry spirals flinging themselves against the low white sky thick as cotton wool. What a blizzard! I expected to see the entire city devastated by such violence.

I climbed up onto the wide sill of the north window of the foyer. It might kill time while I waited to watch the storm among the man-made peaks.

Now the entire city vanished behind a white curtain. No, one skyscraper on the next corner — I could still see it rising thirty, fifty, stories high. I watched it apprehensively. Would its incredible slenderness bend or break before the impact of such a howling furious wind? Its hundreds of lighted windows trembled like yellow tears through their white veils of snow. It remained bravely upright.

Then slowly emerging through the swirling mist loomed a poignant sight. Floating in the snow-laden air appeared the tops of three tall ghostly white shapes. They looked like sailing ships advancing through a fog. I'd never seen anything quite so tremulously beautiful. This was the first winter I had lived sufficiently high above the city to witness its incredible drama of light on the skyscrapers. It changed every hour of the day and night.

A few yellow lights, dancing crazily like small drunken stars, studded these three faint shadowy structures. Were they real or only phantom skyscrapers? The disembodied spirit of architecture made visible? Their beauty struck me like a blow in the chest. I pressed my clenched fist against the sweet pain. Did their very vagueness — like Chinese paintings — suggest illimitable reaches to man's imagination? Lure his spirit to soar far beyond them as mere realistic buildings never could?

The clock struck nine. He was not coming home to dinner. I sat on and on, numb with grief, my body growing numb with cold.

But look, look! Something exciting was happening up at Thirty-third Street, now. Suddenly I could see that slender grey monolith thrusting its head up out of sight into the white mists ascending to who knows what infinite heights. Great white avalanches of snow slid swiftly across its grey facade. Then thin white scarves of mist fluttered across its face. Now you saw the Empire State, now you didn't. Was it so unearthly tall it lived in a world where atmospheric effects unknown to lesser buildings played upon it!

This was like some celestial battle being fought out in the sky. A conflict between the elements and man's handiwork. Again and again the wind-driven sheets of snow wrapped it round in a white shroud of oblivion. I waited breathless each time. Invariably the grey tower emerged free and triumphant. Had not man's art won its battle with the elements?

Enthralled by the witchery of the winter night, I felt a new inexplicable joy beginning to stir in my sore heart.

My numbed spirit, deadened by months of sorrow, slowly began to expand like a cold tight flower bud in a warm room.

Now minute white bullets of sleet struck viciously at the window pane against which I leaned. Cold wind moaning about this twentieth floor found every available crack. The coldness moved through the glass, tangible as a block of ice. But I could not leave this exhilarating drama, this celestial cinema. I might miss something. The climax that might reveal some final secret.

Hastily I took a heavy woolen blanket from the bedroom closet, wrapped myself in it twice over and resumed my observation post. No street was visible from this window, no moving automobiles, or scurrying people, no earth. I was as peculiarly alone in my aerie as an eagle on a lofty mountain crag — above the storm below.

This great throbbing pulsing city — it stopped for nothing — not for wind or ice or sleet, for cold or storm or broken hearts. It lived and rejoiced through anything — everything. Strong — indestructible — triumphant. Did it bade human beings to be the same?

The mad white storm raged on and on. Gradually I felt the wind blow through my own feeble fears, lift my sodden thoughts from the ground till they too seemed to sail through the wintry air. The vulnerable human heart might be deadened but the senses, the mind, the spirit — they were alive even against their own volition.

Exultation, unsought, swept through me like cold clean wind. Suddenly my battered spirit seemed to burst free like a bird too long imprisoned in a cage of sorrow. Out the window it went. Like a white bird of winter it flew not away from the storm but straight into the heart of it. Some vital part of me was winging its way higher and higher through the illimitable milky white void. It soared and circled with delight as if once again in its own element. It joined in the swirling dance of the snow and sleet circling round and round that great skyscraper, growing fainter and fainter until it was indistinguishable from the snow itself.

The very essence of my being, like an undifferentiated snowflake, was incorporated, was made a small part of the great swirling mass of snow, wedded inseparably with the elements caught up in the inexplicable rhythm of the universe...

Time ceased to exist...

Eventually my wild spirit returned to earth as softly as a forgotten snowflake. I rose from my long vigil at the window, scarcely aware of my cramped muscles, filled with a strange peace that passed my understanding. Inexplicably, I felt cleansed of daily pettiness, of recrimination and resentment, bitterness and self-pity, desire to strike back when hurt, free of wounded pride.

That mysterious union with nature had imbued me with a new strength to make one final effort to break through the baffling wall of ice behind which this beloved man was mysteriously dying. And if that failed, it would be a kindness to leave him to wrestle alone with his problem whatever it was. This was the only way I knew to help him, to save him from complete collapse, to save his life perhaps, and my own.

The clock struck eleven. The bridegroom of a few months was not coming home at all tonight. Sleeping at his mother's again probably. I cleared the cold dinner off the table and went to bed but not to sleep.

Questions continued to swirl slowly in my head like snowflakes subsiding after a storm. Were young American girls nurtured on half-truths? Was it true that love and romance and marriage settled all problems for all women?

Did our final happiness lie in attaching ourselves to something larger, more enduring than mutable human beings? Something immutable such as art, or nature, or better yet—to the Unknown — for want of a better name?

CHAPTER 14

SUN AND EARTH

TRANSITION

Years passed. Years of sadness and bewilderment. Years of depression — worldwide and personal. It was the 1930s.

All my life I had relied on the American credo as indestructible — that anyone by her own efforts could save herself from defeat and poverty. Always there was an opportunity waiting.

Now like millions of Americans, I discovered that a college education, years of experience in the business world, eagerness to work — all meant nothing.

Sometimes terror — stark terror — faced me in the night like a burglar standing at the foot of my bed. How, I demanded angrily, could the men who ran the economic machinery of the world bungle the job so tragically? Why should millions of innocent people suffer through no fault of their own?

And as I sat in my lonely little apartment, I struggled to understand — daily — hourly — what had wrecked our beautiful marriage. Grief was a constant companion, sometimes walking beside me quietly, sometimes clutching at me with ravenous fingers. Nevertheless all these black years were faintly yet steadily illuminated by a small white flame of determination never to be defeated by life — no matter what.

Marriage and pain had taught me what wiser women already knew. Without love, life is not worth living. Without a husband a woman feels only half a woman. She is not brave and strong and able to stand alone. She wants a strong man to lean on. Maybe in my particular case, I was nothing but a clinging Southern vine. I had no intention of trying to be anything else.

Once a woman tastes the potential joys of marriage, its companionship, its warmth and enrichment, she longs for the real thing permanently. Freedom was a delusion. Without a close human tie, I realized for the first time, we drift about the earth like rootless thistledown. To be first in somebody's life — that knowledge sustains us through all vicissitudes. And we tire of living only for ourselves. We long to live for someone else. So I remarried.

COUNTRY

My new husband and I spent enchanted weeks on what seemed to us an enchanted island — Bermuda.

We returned to New York. The first day at our hotel, he dropped his bombshell.

"How would you like to buy a house in the country and live there all year around?"

I laughed. This was his idea of humor of course. For we were both incorrigible New Yorkers. He had been born and raised in New York. I was a convert to the city and like all converts a fanatic on the subject.

That afternoon we drove around the winding country roads of Connecticut, looking at houses. I said to myself, what has the country to offer a city person? Isn't it a place of stagnant ponds and stagnant minds? Of insects, flies and mosquitoes and small stinging gossips? Of leaking roofs and snowbound roads and frozen sensibilities? Of artistic apathy and intellectual death? Oh, yes, the country may be fine — for pioneers and farmers. We are neither, thank you.

Finally in a large town my husband spied a white colonial house. It seemed like the country because it was opposite a park with many trees, a river, and a minor mountain with red rock palisades thrusting themselves upward like those along the Hudson. He and the agent drove off to the office of some rival agent for the keys. I rested on the white stone seat in the old deserted garden behind the house.

I sank gratefully to the sun-warmed bench. Then I cast a prejudicial eye about me. Yes, to be honest, it was a lovely old garden — for someone else. A few red flowers of some kind were blooming by the white lattice fence. Pretty — but what of it? Not to be compared to the glorious florist shops in New York. I had never planted a seed in the ground in my life and had no desire to.

BIRD

Suddenly there came a startling swish of wings. A flash of brilliant color cut through the garden's green quietness. It was a large audacious blue bird. He perched himself on the edge of the round marble bird bath. Or was it cement?

This bird was an exhibitionist. Now he was spreading his wings wide to display his beauty. My city-bred ignorance of birds could easily have filled twelve large volumes of Audubon. But this was a blue jay, wasn't it? His arrangement of blue, grey and white feathers was a marvelous piece of intricate workmanship.

Someone had gone to a great deal of trouble to design this bird. Why? For biological reasons or artistic? I didn't know.

Oh, well, why get excited about a mere blue jay. Of no consequence in the scheme of a wonderful life like ours in New York. Yet there was a sort of mystery about a bird that eluded me. What was it?

If you lived in the country — could you discuss the latest books and World War II with birds? Wouldn't I die of loneliness buried alive here in this beautiful green prison?

SQUIRREL

Now a squirrel came flowing down the trunk of a tree. Was he grey or was he brown? How marvelously he matched the bark of the tree. That clever old protective coloration business. Apparently he didn't see me. Wasn't that rather stupid of him? I sat motionless as a statue. He came bounding over the high unmowed grass. Frantically he dug up some buried treasure. Then he sat up on his hind feet. He turned it round and round in his quick front paws with a nervous haste that was positively pathological. Was it an acorn? Or didn't they have acorns in late Spring? I didn't know. My ignorance of such simple fundamental facts of nature appalled me.

He was cunning and all that. But what earthly use would he be if you wanted to give a dinner party where wit and wisdom and wine flowed freely? Like those glorious dinner parties which were one of the chief joys of city life.

I turned my head away. This garden was attempting to take unfair advantage of me. Well, it was futile for sly old lady nature to produce all her bag of tricks. I positively refused to be seduced into living in the wilderness.

TREES

And yet there was something wonderfully sweet about sitting here in this sunny old garden in delicious unaccustomed idleness. In the city everyone crowded eighty seconds worth of activity into every minute.

The flood of yellow warmth continued to pour down on me steadily. I laughed and said to myself, your hungry body absorbs sunshine fast as a *baba au rhum* soaking up its sweet rum sauce.

I stretched my long slender legs out luxuriously. My body felt as contented as a cat. Could idleness be so full — of what? I didn't quite know.

What unutterable peace here. Even nature held her breath. Not a stir of wind now. Not a movement of birds. I sat listening to the unaccustomed silence. It vibrated against my ears like distant music.

Suddenly all the sweet tranquility of the earth was shattered by a horrendous noise. A half dozen airplanes roared and thundered over my head. What if bombs should come hurtling down on this peaceful old Connecticut garden? America wasn't in the Nazi's Fascist war yet but our turn would almost inevitably come soon. We were already busy making munitions for Britain in her tragic plight.

All those lovely living green trees might be destroyed. Men hate each other but who could hate a tree? Pictures of other trees flashed before my memory's eye. You saw them in all the horrible newsreels at the movies. Those gaunt charred skeletons of trees left behind on all the battlefields of England and Europe. I shuddered, sat up straighter and looked at these trees before me with new eyes.

Trees had never been a vital part of my life. Now I gazed intently at a particularly lovely one. Its name was unknown to me.

The longer I looked, the more difficult it was to tear my eyes away. Then an uncanny thing happened. All my life apparently I had seen trees through a thick glass wall. Suddenly the everyday barrier of blind acceptance abruptly fell away. It revealed the eternal wonder of the commonplace.

The tree before me did not **look** any different. It **felt** different to me. I became aware of its alive-ness for the first time in my life. I was drawn over into its non-human world. It did not come over into my human world.

A new perception opened within me like the lens in some powerful new camera. This tree appeared to vibrate the way heat waves vibrate in the distance on a hot summer's day. It stood there throbbingly alive, strong, yet delicate. It emanated a strange kind of power that was almost palpable. It was separate from human life, mysteriously beyond it. Yet it was friendly. If you knew the secret you might draw comforting strength from a tree. It seemd to say: loved ones may die, friends betray you, mankind disillusion you but I — I will never fail you. Trees — trees go on forever. (Forever, if man's devilish bombs did not destroy them!)

Gradually the thick glass wall of ordinary unawareness slipped back into its accustomed place. The tree became just a tree once more. The magic was gone, vanished.

So that was it! Now for the first time in my entire life I faintly understood — **not with my mind but with my emotions** — why the Druids could have worshipped trees. Strange how the threat of losing beauty enhanced its beauty.

SKY

Now my eyes were drawn up beyond the trees to the sky. The usual pale anemic unfriendly Northern sky chilled my spirit. Every day of my life I missed that rich blue heart-warming sky of Texas. But today this one had attained a very respectable shade. In the busy city you never had time to sit and merely look at the sky. Now I actually began to see the sky at which my eyes had been looking for some time. Now it came alive. It too seemed to vibrate just as the green tree had done. I held my breath, waiting. It was going to speak to me, to reveal something stupendous.

Nonsense, reason scoffed. Any scientist will tell you it's nothing but air turned blue by distance and particles of moisture and dirt. How could anyone get so excited about that?

Or was the sky the impenetrable blue veil drawn across the face of infinity? But I didn't believe in infinity, did I?

SUN

The hot heavy hand of the sun continued to press its weight down upon me holding me a motionless captive here in this mysterious garden. I loved it. Like a relaxed luxurious cat, I never wanted to move again as long as I lived.

Now my veins flowed with something thick — fragrant — golden like honey. Could it be sunshine?

The hot rays penetrated my bare arms. They needled into my pores drugging me with a delicious sense of well-being. I did not feel drowsy, I felt teemingly alive, alert, as if every atom of my body danced a little drunkenly.

The flowers opened their petaled cups to catch the flood of sunshine. So my spirit slowly expanded to catch the flood of strange new euphoria pouring into it. All the confused fragments of life, of human life, began to settle quietly into their proper places. Questions too deep for words were being answered.

Now I knew for a fleeting second that life was good — indisputably good! Or could be, if it were not marred by the stupidity of man, the cruelty of wars. When man expanded to his true stature under the caress of the sun, it released the innate good and love dormant in him. Or was this nothing but a moment of relaxed nerves and bodily health?

EARTH

But my feet! What in the world had happened to them? They had been resting contentedly in the long grass below the stone seat. Now I could not move them. They felt heavy as if they were trying to take root in the good earth.

In a city of stone and cement you grew painfully hungry for the feel of the earth beneath your feet without being aware of the nature of your hunger.

Now the shadows of the trees lengthened. They lay long and black across the green grass, across the bench where I sat. But the odor. What was it! Now from all sides a strange provocative fragrance assaulted my nostrils. It rose from the earth. It was disturbing.

Again and again I drew in great deep breaths, filling my lungs full of this earthy pungency. It smelled of decaying leaves and the moist coolness of the soil. The earth at dusk smelled of elemental strength and permanence, of timeless centuries — of eternity.

Suddenly I was struck motionless as though laid under a magic spell. The whole physical world had vanished right away. My body no longer seemed to exist. I felt the firm walls of my individuality crumbling, becoming fluid like a child's candy left out in the sun to melt. Now my personal identity was slowly dissolving. Was I disintegrating, flowing back into the earth from which I originally was created? Was I dying?

Now with each deep intake of that provocative odor I felt, instead, that I was drawing up the strength of the earth into myself. Some dark uncanny force flowed between the earth and me. All barriers melted away while the earth filled and fed me to overflowing, enlarged me — immeasurably; enriched me —

infinitely. It left me fecund and wise-feeling, loving and strong with the simple elemental strength of the good earth, prepared to face life in the country, marriage — war and even death — with a warm smiling serenity...

(We bought the house.)

CHAPTER 15

PAINTING

We walked into the Modern Museum of Art eager with anticipation. It was a loan exhibit of old masters from the Italian government. I forget the date. But it must have been shortly before Mussolini joined Hitler's war. For years my husband and I had haunted the galleries and museums everywhere. Now however, he was too busily engaged in war work to continue his own Sunday painting.

Today there was a crushing crowd. New Yorkers never intend to miss anything important. We inched along in the crowd, but separately. That was always our tacit understanding at exhibits. We met later and compared reactions whose similarity deepened and doubled our individual enjoyment.

I studied the lesser examples of Italian art. I was not swept off my feet, as I had expected to be. Finally I entered the last room. It was packed with people. Most of them were small short dark foreigners — probably home-hungry Italians. I could see over their heads. Oddly enough there was only one painting in this room. Foolishly I assumed this was because the Museum simply had not been furnished with enough pictures by Italy to fill its many rooms. Vaguely my short-sighted eyes could discern that it was a portrait, apparently of a man. How disappointing. I cared less for portraits than any other genre.

Slowly I insinuated myself through the throng. I stood quite close rudely obstructing the view of other people. It was the portrait of a rather homely old man with a long white beard. He was sitting in an ugly armchair and wearing a purple-red cape or was it a chasuble? One incredibly long thin hand rested on something dark on his knee. Was he a cardinal or a pope? I knew nothing of ecclesiastical dignitaries. I did not know who he was nor who had painted him. Never, oh, never did we look at the signature first or even the title. That was against all the rules. We let the picture speak to us first always.

As I looked, immediately — or was it gradually? (I shall never know) — I began to feel odd. A peculiar physical upheaval occurred. My whole insides were turning over. My very organs seemed to be tumbling over each other. The way you see clothes tumbling over each other through the little glass window in an electric washing machine. My heart began to thump harder and harder against my ribs. I held my breath. It was frightening.

It was that picture! Some magnetic current seemed to emanate from it. It was uncanny. That picture was alive. That man was alive — **more** than alive! He was hypnotizing me.

The artist's eye had penetrated through the reserve of this celebrated official's exterior, direct into his hidden brain, his private heart and inmost character. God, it was wonderful. For there was the whole man laid bare before you, mercilessly dissected not by a surgeon's scalpel but by a painter's brush. His secret thoughts and desires exposed. His past history writ large on his face. You understood him better than if you had met him face to face. Better than if you had known him for a lifetime. A clever, capable, brilliant man — firm, forceful, even ruthless and cruel when he deemed it necessary. It was not a condemnatory portrait, it was merely mercilessly truthful.

I continued to stand there held in the hypnotic grip of this astounding picture. What a face! No gentleness, no mercy for the weaknesses of mere mortals, no pity for the mistakes of the poor blundering human race. No, this man's face was thin and sharp and cold, shrewd, crafty, skeptical, intellectual and ascetic. It was a face that said, "I've seen it all. All the follies of men, the chicanery, the hope and pathos." Did a gleam of compassion lurk in the eyes? Certainly none in the thin iron mouth.

And all this was conveyed to your eye and mind merely by color and line, by highlights and shadows! I tell you it was a form of magic. I did not believe the evidence of my own senses.

How long I stood there motionless, mesmerized, allowing this extraordinary picture to work its spell upon me, I do not know. But I know it agitated me more profoundly than all the paintings I ever had seen in my entire life — that was now so full of beautiful paintings — thanks to my husband. But it was **too** overpowering. My inner being was in painful turmoil. I could bear no more. Automatically I glanced at the signature and title and fled from it.

Desperately I sought privacy. I turned my back to the roomful of people. I stared blindly out the window that overlooked the garden of statuary on Fifty-fourth Street. Every atom of my body and mind was shaken out of its customary sluggish state. I stood there dazed, wishing this wonderful frightening sensation would abate. I could not endure to expose my tell-tale face to other people, not even my husband. It was all too intimate — too — too sacred almost — or was it too abnormal?

I heard my husband's voice behind me. "No wonder you stared at that Titian so long. It says here in the catalog that critics consider 'Pope Paul III' the greatest portrait ever painted in the world."

I did not answer. I could not trust my voice. I did not turn my head. My husband threw one startled glance at my face, took my arm firmly and guided me expertly out of the crowded museum. He was warning me constantly that I responded too intensely to every stimulus.

We walked along Fifth Avenue toward his club. I still felt exceedingly strange but happy now. I felt — what? Cleansed! Yes, that was the nearest word I could find to describe this peculiar sensation. Purified. Internally cleansed. The way you feel after a vigorous swim in the ocean when all your inner impurities have been washed away even more thoroughly than the external ones. This portrait of a homely old man actually had subjected me to a powerful internal bath. Who ever heard of such a preposterous thing?

I felt physically relaxed, emotionally serene — somehow pure. I could feel all the old habitual hostilities, the petty irritations in me melting — flowing away, leaving a residue of harmony. It was like a miner washing his pan of gold ore free of dirt in a swiftly flowing river.

I glanced at my husband with new eyes. All the warm beauty of companionship, of marriage, of closeness to another human being rose in me the way water rises in a well. My love flowed out of me toward the man beside me. I laughed, slipped my arm through his and pressed it firmly. He turned and smiled deep into my eyes. I knew he understood. The art of painting had brought us closer together. It had led us into one of those still pools of rapport which constitute the sweetness of marriage.

Was this what Aristotle meant when he said purification was the primary function of art?

CHAPTER 16

MUSIC

Suddenly the houselights dimmed. Quickly I followed the urgent usher, slipped into my seat between the president of our company and my husband. The gleaming gold curtains swept back in vast curving lines — a nice bit of drama in itself. The audience should have applauded. It did when Sir Thomas Beecham appeared. He bowed, then raised his baton.

I had heard this opera several times before right here in the Metropolitan. It was not overpowering. Nevertheless today I squeezed my husband's arm so hard in eager anticipation he groaned aloud. People turned their heads disapprovingly.

It was Ezio Pinza and Grace Moore in Charpentier's *Louise*. In Acts I and II they were pleasant — competent — without passion. That was not enough. We were bitterly disappointed. Finally they came to life.

In the third act Grace Moore became transformed. She ceased to be a nice woman from Tennessee with an excellent voice. She became a young French girl, passionately in love, living with her lover on Montmartre. She began to sing, *"Depuis le Jour."* Her voice was warm, vibrant.

"Since the day I gave myself, all florescent seems my destiny. I seem to be dreaming under a fairy sky, the soul still drunk with your first kiss ... Kiss me ... make me die in thy arms."

You forgot the awkward translation of the libretto for her voice now soared in genuine ecstasy. It sank to a tender caress. Once again its crescendo exulted magnificently. Listening, you were swept away by her and with her. She was what

Julien pronounced her — a symbol of the great city of Paris. The personification of youth, love, eagerness. Julien and Louise ceased to be specific individual lovers, they became all lovers. In the mysterious alchemy of art, the particular became the universal. Paris symbolized all cities.

The fourth act was something I shall never forget as long as I live. Something electrifying had now happened to Pinza, too. He ceased to be a tall handsome Italian. He became not only Le Pere but all loving fathers. He took his daughter on his knee. In that melodious recitative, the *Berceuse*, his voice ached with tenderness. The orchestra breathed out its own haunting melody. Then Le Pere began to plead with Louise to come home.

Tears flowed freely down the faces of this sophisticated cosmopolitan audience.

A passionate family quarrel ensued on the stage. Now singing, music, and acting all fused, rising to such emotional heights it stirred your very bowels. People on all sides were crying unashamedly.

It was the eternal tragedy of parent and child. Everyone who ever had been a rebellious youth or a loving parent had experienced it. Quietly I wept to think of how I had broken my father's heart by leaving him and his home for New York.

The whole audience sat in tense stillness — our petty personal troubles washed away. Pity, as Aristotle says, is a cleansing agent.

Finally, in the last scene Louise looked out the window of her father's garret at the great city stretched out below her.

"Paree! Paree! M'appelle ... Paris, Paris, calls me ... Oh, the magic, the dear music of the town."

Her tones were so exultant they pierced the marrow of your bones. Cold chills ran down my back.

And so the story ended with tragedy for the parents, the loss of their child. It was a sad triumph for the daughter free to pursue a radiant future, to live her own life — not the life of a dependent child.

The houselights came on. Half the audience was blowing its nose and wiping its eyes — a spectacle I did not recall witnessing in this opera house for many a year. All the many years I had lived in New York I had come here every week during the season sitting alone in the topmost balcony, often weeping from excess of pleasure.

Slowly, playing for time, I pinned on my hat. In a daze I powdered my face, renewed my lipstick from sheer habit. I felt as if I had undergone some purifying religious experience more profound than any I ever had experienced in any church.

Eventually I rose and joined the two patiently waiting men. None of us uttered a word. Our moist shining eyes spoke eloquently to each other. The three of us walked up Broadway in a silence electric with feeling. Finally the two men began to laugh and make risque jokes about the women singers to conceal their deep emotion in that strange way Anglo-Saxon men have. But what, I said to myself, was wrong with good honest emotion, for heaven's sake? Didn't the psychologists warn us that the repression of emotions caused trouble?

Now the men were deep in a discussion of war materials. The factory was producing parts for the Army and Navy. The shortage of certain strategic metals was so acute my husband traveled all over the country to find and purchase them.

The exalting effects of the opera continued to expand within me light circles of warm light. Then a great flood of magnanimity for the whole human race swept through me. I knew I loved everybody all of a sudden. Passionately I longed to serve, to sacrifice myself for other people. I who was basically so selfish. It was incredible!

At this moment three planes roared low over our heads. Everyone on the streets stopped abruptly and looked up apprehensively. Might they not be German planes ready to bomb New York? America and England and France were losing the war at a frightening rate. I think it was 1943. We all lived in daily fear, sorrow, and anxiety.

Now I did not turn a hair. All fear of war, death, destruction had miraculously vanished. I, who never had been courageous in my whole life, was filled with courage. I felt strong as never before, adequate for any crisis. I longed to walk calmly about the streets binding up the bloody wounds of the dying, nursing the casualties.

So that was supposed to be one of the secrets of great music — it could ennoble us.

Or was it absurd, unscientific, to believe that mere sound waves passing through the air and entering our ears could open a door within us where lay buried the good, the true, and the beautiful?

CHAPTER 17

DANCING

It happened one night in a musty dusty little old theater in New York. The mystery, the mystical magic of ballet was revealed. It was in an old French film. The tickets were only thirty-three cents. But it aroused me more deeply than any dancing I ever had seen.

Tonight I achieved the mysterious fulfillment on the brink of which the one and only Pavlova had left me trembling time and again when I was a young girl. It left me more breathless than the castanets of Argentina, more deliciously amazed than Shankar and his Hindu dancers.

This film preceded by a year or two the glorious renascence of ballet all over the Western world. It surpassed, incredibly enough, the enchantment I later enjoyed repeatedly under the spell of Danilova and Alonso, Hightower and Markova, de Mille and Boris.

The picture was called *Ballerina*, based on the novel, *La Mort du Cygne*, by Paul Moran. It was the story of the French ballet — laid in the bare ugly behind-the-scenes of the Paris Opera House. It opened very inauspiciously. The heroine, Rose Souris, played by Janine Charrat, was a little girl about thirteen. The French realists showed merciless close-ups of her thin bony knees, angular arms, her coarse homely face as she practiced at the bar on the bare backstage. She was one of the *petite rats*, a pupil in the ballet school.

"I can't look at that homely little brat," my husband said in a loud whisper. "Wake me up if anything interesting happens."

Oh dear, how could I enjoy it if he were bored? Should I offer to leave now? No, wait and give it a fair chance before we walked out.

Gradually something satisfying, if not exciting, commenced to emerge. Little Rose's passion for the beauty of the ballet began to shine through her ugly little face. It made her beautiful — almost, as she enshrined the cast-off slippers of the ballerina, Beaupre, under the glass case where the family clock really belonged.

Beaupre danced several times. It was not exciting. But Rose rushed into their ugly dressing room one morning exclaiming to another *'petite rat'*, "Oh, you should have been here last night. At dress rehearsal **She** danced the Dying Swan. The whole corps was allowed to sit out front and watch." Rose lifted her eyes heavenward and clasped her hands rapturously together. "It was so beautiful, we all cried."

And then something occurred which made me cry. A very young dancer was being tested to displace the older Beaupre. The new dancer was supported by no beautiful backdrop, no fancy lighting. No full orchestra accompanied her, merely a man in shirt sleeves at a piano on a bare hideous stage. And she was dressed not in some lovely *tutu* or enchanting costume. She wore only the simplest, shortest little practice tunic.

This was the first time in my life I had seen a ballet in a motion picture. It was like a different art. You could see everything — all the details, all the nuances, even the facial expression.

Her unsmiling face was solemn, sad, inward-gazing, like the wrapt listening faces of the most dedicated musicians. Yet her body expressed joy. The lovely dancer's thighs swelled like great lily buds. All the movements of her body made one fluid line flowing like water.

This unknown dancer turned and leapt in *grand jetés* defying all the laws of gravity. Her joy in her own body, her warm assurance leapt out at you.

She held her incredible *penche arabesque* as if the perfect balance of the human body could produce the most blissful of all serenities. The thrilling whip of her leg in her brilliant *fouette en tournant* left you breathless.

Slender as a flower, her white tunic clinging like drooping petals, she stood poised briefly in the fourth position *sur les pointes* — sweetly poignant.

But it was that wildly beating foot, like the fluttering of a frightened bird, in her *petite battements* which melted your heart right away. Achingly lovely, tragically ephemeral.

Then without music, the only sound the sibilant scrape of her toes, she moved across the stage in little traveling steps *sur les pointes*. It made something tighten in your chest. It was so lovely it pierced you with sweet pain.

Did not her dancing display all the most beautiful lines of which the human body is capable? But it was tantalizing because so transitory. The beauty of one intoxicating line melted into the next too soon, too soon! Oh, to be a sculptor and catch such elusive beauty permanently in stone.

I leaned over and asked an enraptured neighbor who this young dancer was in real life.

"Mia Slavenska," she whispered in shocked amazement at my ignorance.

So Slavenska danced on and on as though drawing on some mysterious inner resource. Every part of her body an obedient instrument attuned to the same key to create a harmonious symphony of movement. A key unrecognized by me, alas.

Soon, however, I too began to feel the exultation of her mind and spirit as it flowed through her flying limbs. She was so obviously in harmony — rapturous harmony — with herself — her whole self — body, mind, and spirit. It was more than that. She was in harmony with everybody in the world, with everything in the world. You felt it. You knew it.

Now she danced with more intense passion. Now she made me feel what she felt. She banished my fatigue, restored the lost harmony to all my discordant selves. She made me whole again. She made a great wave of warmth expand something sweet within me. I felt a delicious intoxication. It was like the afterglow of champagne — all knots untied — all confusion stilled. You knew life was good — good in spite of war and death and cruelty. Fundamentally life was good — for the species if not always for the individual.

Now something different emanated from Slavenska. Now she seemed to withdraw to another plane, a purer spiritual plane. She seemed to be dancing some religious ritual, celebrating some solemn mystery. She looked as if she were dancing to the inaudible music of some invisible orchestra, moving in harmony with some cosmic principle.

It was so beautiful it hurt. Tears suddenly welled up and stood unshed in my eyes. Tears from the obscurest depths of my being. Now for one blissful moment I lost myself utterly. I felt as if I merged with some great glowing power larger than myself a millionfold. I was lost — diffused — in some golden luminous fog. I was part of it — filled with peace — reassurance — joy — a warm golden expansiveness.

I embraced the whole human race with infinite love. I embraced the unknown mystery beyond it. I knew that mankind was good because I was good because we all were part of the supreme good of the universe.

CHAPTER 18

SCULPTURE

Finally one morning after being in bed nearly two weeks with a wicked virus, I felt faint signs of convalescence. My weak watery eyes wandered to the books in the shelves besides my bed. My hand did not hesitate a moment. As if guided by some uncanny power it selected an old blue book *Art*, by Auguste Rodin. I had purchased it years ago but never read it. Evidently I had anticipated the great day when I might be ripe for it.

It was necessary to support it on a pillow on my abdomen. I opened it indifferently and gazed at the frontispiece — a photograph of *Eternal Spring*, by Rodin. I remembered vividly the first time I had seen this statue. It was in Chicago. I was twenty. I was attending a social service school expecting in one summer to learn how to abolish poverty from the face of the earth.

At the settlement house where I lived, a young professor of philosophy was appalled at my provincialism. So he rushed me to the Art Institute. This was the first museum of any kind to which I ever had been exposed. My companion gazed at the nudes as calmly as if they were chairs. Not the little girl from Texas. I was beholding a nude man, marble or otherwise, for the first time in my life.

It was not Rodin's *Eternal Spring* which stopped me in my tracks. It was Michaelangelo's, *The Captive*, in all his unabashed maleness. Defiantly I planted myself before it. I studied it inch by inch. A dozen devils tortured me. In the provinces where I was raised, sex was considered an instrument of Satan. All the Christian ministers, all the mothers, exhorted us constantly to be ashamed of our own bodies.

But I had read a book or two. I knew this puritanical attitude was not the only one. My body did not know it. I blushed from forehead to foot. My flesh became a battlefield. Obstinately I stood my ground. And for three months afterward I repeated my visits to the Art Institute. But the nudity still obscured the art as far as this little provincial was concerned.

A few years later in New York this same cosmopolitan young man lured me to the Metropolitan Museum. But sculpture left me cold — as cold as the marble from which it was carved. I was at fault, but how? In dozens of museums I continued through the intervening years to stare at hundreds of statues — unmoved.

As I lay in bed today, I studied these amazing photographs of the world's most famous sculpture. Somehow they seemed warmer, more alive than they ever had in the museums. Here was *La Pense*. Victor Hugo. *The Crouching Venus*. And even *The Nike of Somothrace* which had greeted me so victoriously on the stair landing of the Louvre.

I turned the pages, caught a glimpse of a certain piece of sculpture and involuntarily covered it with my hand. It frightened me. It always had. It attracted me, too — irresistibly. I stole another look at it. I shook my head. "I am undone. I am undone." Every time I ever had seen it through the years, in any form, these exact words repeated themselves.

It seemed so final. Beyond it there was nowhere to go. It held the answer to all things — if only we knew what the answer was. What was it? Oh, would I never understand the mystery that animated sculpture?

I removed my hand and studied it again. Reason attacked the problem. Why in the name of heaven should three large women, sitting down doing nothing, minus heads, minus arms, affect anyone so strongly? Was it the enchanting lines of that third reclining figure? Or was it the draperies — those incredible draperies? That multitude of folds, those fluid flowing lines — like swirling water? There was something absolutely hypnotic, unearthly, about them. No ordinary cloth woven by man ever had fallen into such strangely alluring folds.

I pounded my chest repeatedly with open palm. Always, always, the *Three Fates* struck me this way — like a blow in the chest. It was a mystery that was unfathomable. Was it their great breasts? Were they the mothers of the race? Or was it the finality of their pose? For years I had been slightly afraid of them. I still was.

Quickly I closed the book to banish them from view. Then I opened it again — at another photograph.

Ah, here was the most provocative marble bust I ever had beheld! Ripples of remembered pleasure flowed through me like a laughing brook. That time the original was exhibited at the Metropolitan, I had walked around and around it unable to contain myself, deliriously happy like a puppy whose master suddenly comes home. It was Houdon's head of Voltaire.

Dutifully I went off and looked at other sculpture in the French loan exhibit from the Louvre. But again and again I was drawn back irresistibly to this focal point, the Voltaire. I stared at that homely old man with the bald head, the cords in his throat, the thin lips and sardonic smile. Somehow it caused my artificial mask of everydayness, of half-truths, to fall right away. It awakened something asleep in me. Was it my better self? I didn't know.

Yet in the presence of that piece of marvelously carved marble I felt suddenly innocent, eternally young, happy, good. It assured me life was good, people were good if only they'd allow themselves to be. I wanted to dance, to sing. And why not, for heaven's sake?

When victory came in World War I, hadn't people all over the United States rushed out into the streets to dance spontaneously? Hadn't they sung and laughed and kissed each other in genuine affection? Why not celebrate beauty? Why not dance and sing in honor of a great victory in art? People even laughed and shouted at lesser things like football games!

I studied the faces of the people thronging through the crowded rooms of the museum. Why did most of their faces appear so expressionless? The marble head of this Frenchman dead nearly two hundred years was more alive than these dignified New Yorkers. Couldn't society function unless everyone restrained his natural emotion, action, and even his words? Was something wrong with our so-called civilization of the twentieth century? Did it inhibit us all too much under the erroneous conceptions of maturity and etiquette?

A child was more honest than an adult. When he was happy, a child danced and sang and hopped about. Why was it forbidden us? I gripped my rolled-up catalog fiercely to restrain my delicious natural impulses to dance and shout.

Suddenly I felt something like a strong electric current touch me. I looked through the crowd far across the room directly into my husband's eyes. He was smiling at me indulgently as a man smiles at a child or an adult in whom the eternal child appears with laughing face. He was the most decorous and reserved of men. Did he think I was revealing my pleasure too much? Wasn't the lack of enthusiasm the one quality from which many moderns suffered keenly? "Enthusiasm" — the word the wonderful wise Greeks coined to mean "possessed by the Gods." Could it possibly derive from the primal source of life? Was that what made a great artist? Was that why, if anyone met life with enthusiasm, people approached to warm their cold hands at his fire, till he saw the spark lighted in their eyes?

Now I returned to the book open on my pillow. Toward the end of the volume, I saw a photograph of the statue of a woman which had baffled me all my life. Whenever I saw a reproduction of it, or even the original in Paris, I asked myself why the critics pronounced this the finest of all classical masterpieces.

Honestly, I said to myself, I simply don't get it. Look at her. She's overweight, her dress is falling off, her arms are broken, her face isn't very pretty even. What is it about this *Venus de Milo* that escapes me?

Baffled for the hundredth time, I continued to stare at it today. Suddenly

I saw not an immobile marble woman but a living moving woman — dancing. Mia Slavenska in her thrilling dance in that cheap little movie of Moran's *Ballerina*. *Venus de Milo's* serenity was the same as that of the dancer's. Why even a blind man could see that this Greek woman had achieved the same peace, the same kind of harmony with herself, with the world about her and even — yes, even with the unknown which surrounds us. So that was it! That explained why it was a masterpiece! Great sculpture can reveal the life principle, and man's relation to it.

Understanding brought such joy that a tide of warmth surged through me. I grasped the blankets in convulsive hands, clamped my teeth together, pressed my eyelids tight and waited. Waited till this wave of elation sweeping through my whole body should subside.

Finally the tension was released. I fell back against the pillows — satisfied — happy.

But reason, suppressed for many months, struggled to rear its ugly head again prepared to refute everything I had felt, even this truth at which I had arrived intuitively on the swift stream of emotion.

Quickly, defiantly, I sought confirmation in the great French sculptor, Rodin.

"When a good sculptor models a torso, he not only represents the muscles, but the life which animates them — more than the life, the force which fashioned them... In the works of Michaelangelo, the creative force seems to rumble..."[1]

"In the majestic rhythm of the outline, a great sculptor, a Phidias, recognizes the serene harmony shed upon all nature by the divine wisdom; a single torso, calm, balanced, radiant with strength and grace, can make him think of the all-powerful mind which governs the world..."[2]

"True artists are the most religious of men."[3]

"The three fates of the Parthenon — their pose is so serene, so august, that they seem to be taking part in something of enormous import that we do not see. Over them reigns the great mystery, the eternal Reason whom all nature obeys and of whom they are themselves the celestial servants... So all the masters advance to the barrier which parts us from the Unknowable."[4]

CHAPTER 19

ARCHITECTURE

GOTHIC

Our distinguished guest from New York arrived on Saturday morning. How could I entertain her? The most interesting sight in our town was the university buildings.

I drove her around the back streets. I must approach those exquisite buildings on Grove Street at the proper angle — from the west.

Only last week I had driven by them late one afternoon. The impact of their unexpected beauty disarmed me utterly. The street curved inward at one place. From that vantage point you could see the whole long lovely length of them all at one time. They extended two full blocks and were three stories high. These two beautiful buildings of rose tapestried brick were the Graduates building and the Sterling Law. In the rays of the late afternoon sun they glowed mysteriously with melting warmth. An architectural triumph in color.

They reminded me of the pink marble of the Grand Trianon in Versailles. Or was it the Petite Trianon (if the Germans had not bombed it out of existence already)?

My startled eyes had gazed at these structures incredulously. Were they not the feminine embodiment of the spirit of youth? It was like being confronted unexpectedly by an extraordinary pretty young girl or handsome youth. Before such pure beauty, all your defenses went down — down. It imbued you with a powerful urge to protect them from all danger, all pain. Even to sacrifice your life if necessary. My grandmother always contended that was the way Southern aristocrats felt about their stately mansions in the Civil War. Does danger, death, and war increase our awareness of beauty? I wondered.

We now arrived at Grove Street. I felt sick with disappointment. Those two pink buildings had the **morning** light **behind** them. Light was the bride of architecture. Would I never learn?

I parked the car and we began our tour of the university buildings on foot. In High Street the Sterling Library and its great Gothic window stopped us in admiration. Then we passed into its stone-cool interior. Involuntarily we both paused. This was not a library at all. It was a vast Gothic cathedral. The great corridor was like the high vaulted nave of some colossal church. What better repository for books? I could not resist showing my friend the card index and how many copies of my own book the library had stocked. We were enchanted by a thousand other fascinating architectural details.

Then we strolled along High Street, our eyes frantically endeavoring to see everything at once. Occasionally the playful spirit of the architects was noticeable. Quaint little men of lead inset at random in casement windows, a carved hand holding a light aloft.

We walked along beside the famous Harkness Tower. It was nothing but an enormous block of grey-yellow stones. We were too close. Was there no vantage point where the onlookers could gain the right perspective? All these magnificent buildings were regretfully crowded together in the very center of the city.

I walked my friend to the end of the block, turned and looked back. Now a thing of heavy stone was transformed by distance into lyric grace. It rushed upward toward the sky like a great Gothic spire. Its vertical buttresses enticed your eyes higher and higher, past story upon story of arcaded windows, toward the tenuous pinnacles delicate as lace work, above the small regal crown, on up where the converging lines continued invisibly, pointing toward some final focal point in space.

We stood silent staring. This beautiful Gothic spire seemed to radiate electrical impulses. It agitated me physically.

Finally the Doctor broke the tense silence. "You remember Henry Adams in his *Mont-Saint-Michel and Chartres?* He says Gothic is the only architecture in the world that gives the effect 'of flinging its passion against the sky.' "[1]

It flings our passion against the sky, too, I thought. I was doubly moved. By the aspiring vertical spirit of this famous spire. And by the discovery of a woman who responded so enthusiastically to this architecture I loved with a blind passion.

"Who did you say the architect of Harkness Tower was?"

"I didn't," I replied, "but it's Rogers. James Gamble Rogers. He designed all the Yale buildings I like best."

We strolled back along High Street. Soldiers were drilling behind locked gates on the old campus. It was horrifying that young boys anywhere in the world must be trained to kill and be killed. Would men never become really civilized? We felt guilty as women that fine young men like these students should be forced to die to protect us.

"But Doctor, does the beauty of all these wonderful Yale buildings help these boys to face death?"

"Ah, that's the $64 question. All art is therapeutic of course. It helps to bring serenity. And if all people could engage in more art, eventually it might destroy the desire for war."

"That anthropologist, Dr. Margaret Mead," I commented, "wrote a most provocative article in the Yale Quarterly. She said the Balinese were the happiest race of people in the world. She attributed it to their daily participation in the various arts. She said it released their unconscious tensions. Isn't that exciting?"

We turned around and faced in the opposite direction.

"Oh, look at that marvelous Gothic arch across the street!" I cried. "The High Street Gateway, I think they call it. Let's go through it."

We stood motionless, however. The grace of that lovely pointed arch was inexplicably moving. It was deeply recessed with rows of intricate carvings. The wrought iron gate was silhouetted jet black against the dazzling white building in the sunlit quadrangle beyond it. Its beautiful diaper pattern stood out boldly like heavy black embroidery on a white background. Above the gateway ran a row of small canopied niches. Somehow they set their seal on the whole with an air of satisfying finality that ran right down to the soles of your feet.

Surely this was the consummation of all gateways. You asked for nothing beyond it. It seemed the culmination of something — you scarcely knew what. You stood motionless contemplating it. Suddenly you knew that because this Gothic arch was perfect, your life, for one glowing moment — however fleeting — was also perfect.

The tide of pleasure was rising steadily but reason thrust itself upward like an obstructing rock. "Why?" I asked. "Why is a Gothic arch so much more — more thrilling than a Roman arch, for instance?"

"Because it does not swing the eye back again like the semi-circular arch," the psychologist explained. "All Gothic lines carry the eye upward. They're full of promise. Possess a quality of infinite aspiration."

Now I was all but bursting with accumulated excitement. Reasons — weren't they almost as stimulating as beauty itself?

We roamed about without any definite objective, looking, talking, admiring. Several times we became lost in the maze of interesting buildings and dead-end quadrangles.

GEORGIAN

Finally we strolled idly across York Street and entered another attractive gate, unaware that we were approaching the culmination of a long glorious morning. We walked slowly, even a little wearily, along a charming flagged walkway. It was walled in on one side by DKE House, and Davenport College on the other, enhanced by tall trees. We watched their shadows dancing on the flagstones. It aroused delicious poignant sensations.

Never satisfied with beauty alone, I insisted on rational explanations.

"Because," the psychologist said, "it gives one a feeling of security, of intimacy, even of romance."

Any woman who knew the answer to abstract questions of aesthetics was more phenomenal than the most beautiful architecture in the world.

The flagstone walk was leading us to a large secluded courtyard whose existence I never even had suspected. Under the arched entrance we stopped and looked up for the first time. A great magnificent red and white tower far across the vast quadrangle struck us speechless. It stood there like a proud young queen with her head held high against the pale blue New England sky. It looked vibrant with the brilliant morning sunlight full on its face.

Distance certainly lent enchantment to this view. I recalled my discovery of a cardinal rule of architecture. A building should be viewed from a certain distance, at the best angle, in the right light. Then all the beauty of its lines and mass, its colors and contours — seemed to fuse, to rise up like an emanation and cast a magical aura about it. Move ten feet nearer, or ten feet to the side, and the magic vanished — like that!

Now our eyes drank in the baffling beauty of that majestic white window. It was arched and tall above a balustraded stone balcony, set like a jewel in the center of the vast expanse of the red brick wall of this spacious square tower. The whole was crowned by an exquisite cupola vividly white in the sunshine, capped by a small gold dome, glittering in the morning light.

Suddenly this great Georgian tower of Pierson College seemed to sway. Or was I dizzy? Had my eyes drunk in too many intoxicating sights in one morning? Surely, I thought, beyond this, Georgian architecture cannot go. Surely this is the ultimate in balance, in beauty, in perfect proportions. The very apotheosis of harmony.

In its presence all the usual barriers between animate man and inanimate things magically melted away. The full tide of beauty flooded all my senses. For one blissful moment I knew the thing I sought was found, the ideal I pursued like a will-o'-the-wisp was here embodied. No longer was I filled with doubts, with questionings. No longer was I afraid — of war — of death — of anything.

For as the sick are said to be miraculously cured at the mysterious shrine of Lourdes, so now did this glorious architectural structure cure my painful incompleteness, its unity make one again the disparate parts of my being.

Then — then as I remained there hypnotized by this resplendent red and white tower, the final, impossible, indescribable occurred. It stopped my breathing, it stopped my thinking.

For suddenly a window opened in the blue sky beyond the tower. Not a real window but a vista of understanding so convincing it seemed visible. Through it shone a light — a dazzling unearthly light.

For one long ecstatic second I felt I could see into the unseen, the unseeable, into the eternal mystery. A flash of intuitive insight revealed to me the nature of things. I apprehended that above and behind everything, beyond good and evil, there exists a vast impersonal order in the universe. A system of cosmic laws on which man can rely, by which he can fashion his life, in which he can immerse himself and be refreshed in time of deepest need.

Man is not alone in an unfriendly universe. Not even modern warring diabolically destructive man is alone. Through beauty he can rediscover and restore his own perennial clarity of vision, his inherent integrity, and his own inner guide to right and wrong.

I saw that through the beauty of great art, we can tap the ultimate source of all good through the awakened good in ourselves.

I saw that beauty proved the existence of what the philosophers called Ultimate Reality, and the religious called God.

CHAPTER 20

DRAMA

It was a cold winter night in the Connecticut hills when this drama occurred. It was the culmination of a hundred preceding dramas on the legitimate stage.

Like most theater goers, I had sat for years expectant — of entertainment and relaxation — and more. Were we not all searching unconsciously for some mysterious release and fulfillment through the play on the stage?

For years I had sought it eagerly in the glorious performances of Eugene O'Neill and Maxwell Anderson and Tennessee Williams. In Shaw and Shakespeare and revivals of Ibsen. The Irish plays and players, the English and the Russian.

I had sat enthralled under the spell of Lawrence Olivier and Vivien Leigh, Lunt and Fontanne, Tandy and Cronyn, all the Barrymores, Meredith and Ahern, Evans and Massey, Hayes and Cornell and Le Gallienne.

Undoubtedly what I sought was there. I was not ripe for it. Or must we be a performer rather than a spectator to taste its full flavor?

I went on a modest lecture tour — in New York City and throughout Connecticut. My audiences usually were groups of college women. The subject was, What the Seven Arts Can Do For You. I was so carried away by my recent ecstatic experience with the arts, I was eager to share them with others. The climax came that night at Naugatuck.

The American Association of University Women asked me to speak to them. It was a bitterly cold night. Too cold to undergo so long a ride through the hill country. My husband offered to drive me.

As the car rushed through the black icy night, I strove to relax, to forget myself, submerging like a submarine into the depths of my subject. Why waste their time with superficialities? Why not plunge down to elemental truths?

We approached the new school on the hilltop where I was to speak. My husband had planned to while away this hour while I talked by attending a movie. At the last minute he dropped his bomb.

"I've never heard you lecture. I'd like to hear you tonight, if you don't mind."

My heart strangled my throat. Oh, Lord, would his critical presence chill my ardor? He was my severest critic when it came to manuscripts. Frequently he placed an unerring finger on the root of the trouble but with a businesslike directness that made my feelings quiver like Jell-O. He never cushioned the blow with praise first.

"If — you think you'd really enjoy it, I — I'd be glad to have you," I lied feebly.

He sat on the back row, the only male present. New England audiences do not accept you with open arms. Invariably at first there is that chilling period of skeptical appraisal of the speaker.

I smiled at them hoping this would thaw the ice a little. It didn't. As university women, I told them, I was certain they themselves had been visited by many wonderful experiences with the arts. (I wasn't certain at all. I knew little about them at this time. But if I had undergone the glories, why not they? No one is unique.)

I launched into an exuberant description of the opera, *Louise*, and its exciting effects; then of Titian's Pope Paul III and how it had cleansed me until I loved the whole world.

As I stood there it felt deeply satisfying to be utterly honest for once, to reveal the most cherished treasures of my thought and feeling, to be my real self for an hour, to discard the polite conventions which conceal us like ugly clothes, to toss away the superficial half-truths of everyday social intercourse, to speak the truth at last.

I talked on and on. I did not grow weary, I did not grow hoarse. I did not stop to drink the water standing on the table. I did become too warm. I did not care. I felt wonderful — as if a green tight bud inside me was slowly expanding into some wonderful full-blown blossom.

I was too vain to wear my glasses. I was too nearsighted to see the expression on my husband's face as far away as the back row. But I was sure if anything were wrong, I should feel it like a stream of icy air. The atmosphere in the whole room now seemed warm — glowing — vibrant.

I relived, reenacted, the emotional storm generated by Swinburne's poem of poems when I was twenty-five. I attempted to recreate in them the conviction it produced of the equilibrium of the universe. I described Mia Slavenska's dancing, its spiritual message. I confessed my former ignorance concerning *Venus de Milo*.

Now I could feel elation dancing in my blood. It was not the sensation of having my head in the clouds, but rather as if I had thrust my roots deep, deep down into the earth. I felt like a tree offering them the natural fruits of the earth. A feeling of kinship with my fellow beings warmer than I ever had felt in my life ran in my veins like sweet sap.

A half dozen faces in the audience now shone like the morning sun. Their eyes glowed with the fire of their own inner warmth. All their own innate goodness, purity and innocence rose to the surface. It dazzled me. I could scarcely endure to look at anything so defenseless. Yet my gaze returned irresistibly to the beauty of character revealed in the responsive eyes of some of those women. Several faces looked literally transfigured.

I tried to convey some semblance of the indescribable joy of creating art yourself such as I had tasted when I wrote my second book. I described the Pierson tower and how through architecture on rare occasions we might catch one blinding glimpse into the order of the universe. It was like some deep religious experience, I said. Such moments could bring us a peace beyond our understanding, a serenity, and a sense of security of which bedeviled, bewildered, modern man — and woman — were so desperately in need.

Having no frame of reference except my own experiences, I suggested that art and religion were closely allied because they probably sprang from the same source — our unconscious minds.

As the hour drew to a close I was startled to feel great waves of love for these people seated in the audience sweeping through me. I always considered myself selfish, self-centered. But now I was suffused with love for old and young, pretty and plain, rich and poor. Catholic and Protestant, Jew and Negro. It was sexless — all embracing — universal. I loved the whole world.

I felt like a great mother. I, who was tall and slender, felt as large and deep-bosomed as Ethel Waters. Some of these women were older than I. They seemed like my children. I longed to solace their sorrows, soothe their worries, help them realize the best that was in themselves.

If the beautiful new school building had burst into flame at that moment, I should gladly have sacrificed my life to save them. I loved my fellow beings better than myself — at least for one brief ecstatic hour.

When the lecture ended, many came up to speak to me. A few clasped my hands with such eager warmth I scarcely could hear the words they said, "You were absolutely **inspired!**" Their faces, their glowing eyes spoke more eloquently than all the fine words in their vocabulary. And I knew I should feel an indestructible bond with these responsive women the rest of my life. No matter how our politics or religion, finances or races, or ages might differ.

My sponsor introduced my husband to the others. Never had I seen him so animated with strange women.

Finally we left and returned to the icy cold car. With exceptional solicitude my husband tucked the carriage robe snugly around my feet. He returned to his side, started the car and we drove away. No comment. I could endure the suspense no longer.

"Well, what did you think of my lecture?"

His voice was low, warm, urgent. "I was enraptured."

I sat back, I was content, fortified now to face any calamity whatever came. We drove in silence.

It was eleven o'clock at night. Half an hour later we were approaching the house of friends in the country. Their lights were still burning so my husband turned into their driveway.

"Well," he announced after they had furnished him with a scotch and soda, "after being married all these years, I fell in love with my wife all over again tonight. I heard her lecture on the seven arts. I thought she charmed them all. I never really understood her until tonight. She's the only person I ever knew in my life who is absolutely — what's the right word? — absolutely **pure.**"

That beautiful speech was enough to nourish me for a year.

During the drive home a bitter wind blew. A tooth that had been gnawing me with a slight periodic pain began to throb. We arrived home at midnight. For three hours I walked the floor with a more excruciating pain than I ever knew existed. It was the first toothache I ever had in my life. It proved to be an abscessed tooth which was extracted the next day.

But that night I walked back and forth — across my bedroom, through the bathroom into the guest room and back again — a hundred times. The pain was indescribable, absolutely unendurable, and yet somehow I wanted to laugh, to sing. In some strange way my pain seemed remote as if it were happening to someone else. Ordinarily I would have telephoned the doctor in the middle of the night, implored him to rush over immediately and give me an injection to stop this agony. I did nothing.

It was too fascinating an experience to forego. It was as if some wall of glass existed between me and the pain. Was it only because I was so thoroughly relaxed after my talk? Even at the dentist, if I relaxed, the pain was far less. Relaxation is a strange thing — it diminishes all kinds of pain but increases all forms of pleasure. But so does stimulation.

In spite of this unholy pain tonight I was possessed by a peace of mind that truly passed my feeble understanding, a sense of permanent security as if I were being cradled in great cosmic arms. There was no urge to analyze it rationally — then. I felt quietly ravished — deeply — thoroughly — in every part of my being. What it all signified — if anything — I did not care — until later.

All my life I had heard that exultation could nullify acute physical pain. I gave no credence to it. But it could. It did. I was still incredulous. Or was it spiritual exultation? In this scientific age how were we to know if we had a spirit or what it was even? Darwin and the scientists and the French Enlightenment had done their best to deprive the human race of a soul. We were all supposed to worship reason.

The following morning when the maid brought up my breakfast tray, she smiled broadly. "I don't need to ask if your lecture was a success last night. Your eyes are still shining. Even your teeth are shining. You look exalted." (She was an ardent Catholic.)

Then another surprising thing happened. For years all the critics announced with finality that the arts were incapable of moving us to moral action. My cook was a nervous high-strung strong-minded woman nearing fifty — unmarried and avidly religious. Fundamentally she was a fine woman. Nevertheless she and I had fallen into several regrettable altercations. She never had worked before for anyone except millionaires with a staff of six to twelve servants. Our mode of life was not sufficiently formal to merit her approval. Frequently she informed me that this or that was not "correct." It was difficult to make her understand that I knew too much about conventional correctness and was struggling toward that coveted stage of freedom where not society, but I, made my own rules.

Now a feeling of genuine empathy, of affection arose in me. I wrote her a long, kind, and what I hoped would be, a helpful letter. A letter, because she could talk louder, longer, and faster than I any day in the week. All the training in the world could not subdue or alter her natural dominant temperament.

It worked a miracle — for a whole month. She exerted noble visible efforts to maintain our beautifully harmonious relationship. It was as if the weight of the world had rolled off my shoulders.

I had first submitted the letter to the critical eyes of my husband. He approved. He himself had been irritated by the behavior of a certain man in business. He promptly went to his desk and wrote a sincerely understanding letter to this difficult person. It improved the situation remarkably — for a couple of weeks.

That evening in Naugatuck had lifted our marital relationship to a plane of tenderness and gentle playful humor that promised to be permanent — if not constant.

By their fruits you shall know them.

CHAPTER 21

LOVE

MARRIAGE

This is marriage: the end of long waiting, this balm that heals years of yearning, this peace that goes down to the depth of being and quiets the troubled waters of the soul.

Does not his man's mind encompass my mind? Does not my woman's tenderness cover him like a cloak?

Man is strong and swiftly I seek his protection. Man is but a child and I am woman, the eternal mother. My breasts are soft for his weary head and troubled spirit.

Marriage is a refuge from the storms of misfortune, the cold winds of life.

The two threads of our lives are interwoven inextricably into a newer and subtler pattern.

It is a mighty chord of music and the days of our lives move to the sound of that harmony.

We are like two trees transplanted side by side, separated to the eye but in the dark underground of our beings grown together forever in a strange dual oneness.

LOVE

When you're ecstatically in love
Miracles are simple daily affairs,
You walk on air
Light as the down of a dandelion
Blown by a summer breeze

Your feet no longer aware of the earth
Your body no longer in need of food.
Love, like a private sun,
Lights up the greyest days,
Love fills the air with the fragrance
Of unknown flowers
Lends strange new beauty
To old accustomed ugliness
And you walk through the streets of life
To the muted music of unseen instruments.

Love suffuses your entire being
With vibrant happiness — intense to the point of pain,
With anguish — poignant to the point of sweetness.
Love lends you (temporarily)
Eternal youth and imperishable beauty,
A new confidence and a new humility.
All the world loves a lover they say
But suddenly, you the lover,
Find yourself loving the whole intractable human race
With a magnanimity
You deemed reserved only for saints.

When you're rapturously in love
You become self-less to an incredible degree
Serving another tastes sweet beyond belief
You long to prove your love
To immolate yourself
To nourish him in health
And nurse him in sickness
You long (almost) for him to fall desperately ill
You dream of abjectest poverty
So you may make woman's supremest sacrifice
Prostitute yourself to save his life.

Love banishes all fears of all things — even death
You may stand on nature's mountain peak
And survey the earth below
Or on man's tallest building of buildings
In the noblest city of cities
And look down at the unconsidered world beneath
And you laugh — exultant
If an atom bomb crashed about you
If the whole known universe were destroyed

Before your very eyes
You would merely laugh — unafraid —
Eager to embrace the ultimate experience
To die at this moment of bliss
Hand in hand with your love,
For what has life to offer you?

You have known love.

PASSION

I

Have you never heard of Woman's Song of Ecstasy?

I am a **flower** — heavy with amorous perfume — opening wide voluptuous petals under the strong sun of his passion, his eyes and lips and hands a swarm of hungry bees that sip and rifle me of all my honey.

I am the **earth** — the parched and hungry earth. When his kisses rain upon me, joy floods the farthermost reaches of my being; every remotest little rivulet is fed, when the tide of ecstasy rushes inland.

I am a soft **couch** to man's weariness, the fountain wherein he renews his youth, the earth wherein he is buried to rise to new life again. Woman is the shrine wherein man communes with his god.

And I am a **child,** an eternal child born into the morning of the world. An innocence lies upon me that a thousand years of kisses could not remove.

I mate naturally like the dryads and nymphs. I am elemental in my instinct and desire. Pagan pure and simple. A high priestess serving the great god Ecstaci.

Man is my **lover** and my child. I am mistress and mother all in one. With his lips at my breast, I would to God I could nourish him — with my milk, my blood, — my soul and my life, if need be — anything — everything — to comfort him, the eternal child.

To be subdued, to be a mere nothing — his plaything, to lose myself in him, my master, there is no joy like that! When his face lies close against mine and I breathe in his hot breath, I am but a bit of clay, and he is a god breathing the breath of Life into me, and then...

... and at last, in that final moment of white heat we become one, my senses no longer able to distinguish my limbs from his limbs, myself from himself — united, irrevocably and forever. The twain shall be one flesh godlike — hermaphroditic like the original gods of man — a dual oneness.

II

Have you never heard the Special Plea for Puritans?

Desire though it spring from the soil, may be made to flower. Were you never able to forget the earth in which it had its birth? Though music comes from bits of wood and wire, do you love music the less for that?

Did not the wine of your senses quicken even your mind to new life and thought? Could your spirit, housed in a body which trembled with such ecstasy, remain untouched, unmoved? By the violent storms in your being was not the very soul loosed for one awful instant from its mooring in the flesh?

Did you feel nothing of a striving after the unattainable, after the unknowable? Oh, did you not soar beyond the limits of human thought? Unite with infinity? Dissolve in the universe? Return into the womb of time whence you came and whither you long always to return?

III

Have you then never heard woman's Song of the Afterglow?

Peace — ah, this blessed peace! I am at peace with myself, with all the world; imperturbable as Buddha. Such calm pervades my being that fire nor flood, disease nor death, could disturb me now. If the millennium should come and I were flung this instant over the edge of the world — I should merely laugh!

And over the still dark pool of my content, intermittent laughter dances like sunlight. Radiant and blooming am I, like a full-blown rose in midsummer. All the restless body quieted. All the discordant nerves vibrate no more. All is sweet, silent harmony.

Magnanimous, generous, I feel patient and kind. All my dormant virtues shrinking under the acids of denial now burst gloriously into full blossom.

And the great and formidable world — ah, see, I weigh it in the palm of my little hand — so! It is to me but a child's plaything. I toss it up and catch it at my will — so! For I am a woman fulfilled. A wife complete, and whole — in harmony with myself, with my fellow beings — in tune with the infinite!

CHAPTER 22

SUMMER

REBELLION

"Damn it, I'm tired of being a gentleman," my husband protested. "I'm sick of dressing up like little Lord Fauntleroy every night. For seven years I've dressed for dinner every night all summer long at that big seaside hotel. I've groomed myself within an inch of my life before I dare step out of our room."

My husband's outburst left me speechless. We were driving home from Boston. He had gone there on business and I had accompanied him. It was April (1950), the time of year hotel reservations for the coming summer must be confirmed.

"Just for once I'd like to get up in the morning and not have to shave. I'd like to putter around the house in my old clothes. I'd like to eat a meal without servants breathing down my neck every minute. I'd like to sit at the breakfast table as long as I liked and read my newspaper without having to consider the staff. Sometimes I'd like to eat crackers and milk for dinner instead of a seven course meal with all the trimmings."

Anger ran over me like a flame. Then remorse made me weak.

"Next summer I'll take you to Europe," he continued. "If only for this coming summer you'd be willing to take a small simple cottage at the seashore. No servants — for Pete's sake. I'll fix the breakfast. You can fix the lunch. And we'll go out to dinner. We can surely get a cleaning woman in. Because I wouldn't want you to soil your lily white hands with a mop. I realize no Southern gentlewoman ever does housework but it wouldn't kill you just for one summer, would it, dear?"

"Well," I replied, "I always thought you enjoyed a luxurious summer hotel as much as I did and wearing evening clothes. It was very stupid of me not to have sensed your attitude long ago. You have been extremely generous, dear. Turn about is fair play."

That was what I said. That was what I thought. It was not what I felt. I was in a turmoil. If, I thought, we take a small cottage, how can I write with him in the next room banging on his typewriter, making all those noisy long distance business calls every five minutes? How can I concentrate for more than two consecutive minutes if I have to answer tradesmen ringing the door bells all day long? The grocer boy, the milkman, the laundry man, the garbage man, the mailman, the electric man to read his meter, the gas man to read his meter, peddlers, neighbors, callers! My poor book! It will be ruined — ruined! And just when I've started to write again after so many months of unproductivity. Oh, God what **am** I going to do?

We looked at seashore cottages on Cape Cod from Falmouth to Chatham. We found nothing suitable. My husband said he would return alone in a couple of weeks.

Gradually as we drove along the Cape in sight of the sea a voice long suppressed within me began to speak like a traitor: For once in my life, **I'd** like to get up in the morning and not have to take a bath, not have to comb my damned hair. I'd love to look down someday and see a run in my stocking and say to hell with it and leave it there. I'd like to look at my nails and let the dirt stay there. I'd like to walk around without a girdle and sit on my backbone.

I was horrified at myself. What was wrong? Did polite society impose too many restraints on our natural animal selves? Certainly for a well-bred woman to scratch her head even in private or pick her teeth, yawn or stretch in public — wasn't that equivalent to being found drunk in a gutter?

HOME

When we arrived home, I gazed at our house with guilty eyes. The crimson drawing room, the blue and white hall, the dining room paneled in Adam green. The lovely crystal chandeliers, the barrel-back chairs like great blue seashells, the delicate curves of the Hepplewhite chairs and the long graceful sideboard.

Oh, God, I loved it! It was my child, my creation! How could I betray it?

I wrote on my book every morning. Exhausted one afternoon I lay down on the Duncan Phyfe sofa in the living room. Where could I put up my feet? Not on the red and gold satin stripes of the sofa certainly. Not on the leather-topped coffee table. Then where? Nowhere!

Never could we put our feet upon a table. It would scratch the polished surface. Never could we tie back a curtain. It would wrinkle it. Nor leave a window open above the glass ventilators at night. It might rain in and ruin the expensive silk draperies. Never leave the shades up on the south to let the glorious sun pour in. It faded the rugs and delicate bedspreads. Never could we sit on the edge of a bed. It would ruin the springs. Never sit on the arm of a chair.

It would loosen it. Never come in with muddy shoes on the immaculate blue carpet.

"Eternal vigilance is the price of liberty," they said. Was eternal discomfort the price of beauty? Were we too civilized?

But in the name of heaven, I had spent years, we had spent thousands of dollars decorating this house! I had agonized for months trying to train servants to take proper care of our precious possessions. A dust brush dropped carelessly on a table could leave a dent in it. A wet can of furniture polish set on a piano could mar it forever. A dirty-bottomed parcel-post package left on pale pink bedspreads could spoil a whole bedroom set. A vacuum cleaner banged against a table leg could scar it for life. Oh, the care, the anxieties, the grief at every disfigurement on the face of beauty. What was the solution?

REBIRTH

Then the most incredible thing happened — the most frightening, beautiful, important experience of my entire life. I understood absolutely nothing of its meaning at the time. I did not even include it in this, my autobiography. Was I too ignorant of its significance, too afraid that others would not believe it? Did I fear it indicated that I was queer — or worse? I honestly do not know.

One morning I was writing at my desk in the quiet writing room of our quiet house in Connecticut. Suddenly everything within my sight vanished right away. No longer did I see my body, the furniture in the room, the white rain slanting across the windows. No longer was I aware of where I was, the day or the hour. Time and space ceased to exist.

Suddenly the entire room was filled with a great golden light, the whole world was filled with nothing but light. There was nothing anywhere except this effulgent light and my own small kernel of the self. The ordinary "I" ceased to exist. Nothing of me remained but a mere nugget of consciousness. It felt as if some vast transcendent force was invading me without my volition, as if all the immanent good lying latent within me began to pour forth in a stream, to form a moving circle with the universal principle. Myself began to dissolve into the light that was like a great golden all-pervasive fog. It was a mystical moment of union with the mysterious infinite, with all things, all people. It was a confrontation with Ultimate Reality, an overwhelming indescribable experience, the ecstasy so intense it was unbearable, the rapture so sweet it was ineffable.

I WAS REBORN

It was the grand perfect purgation, I was washed clean and pure like a sea-shell by the mighty tides of the sea. All my personal problems fell away out of sight. My ego had drowned in boundless being. Irrefutable intimations of immortality came welling up. I felt myself becoming an indestructible part of indestructible eternity. All fear vanished — especially fear of death. I felt death would be the beginning of new more beautiful life. There was no death.

Extraordinary intuitive insights flashed across my mind. I seemed to comprehend the nature of things. I understood that the scheme of the universe was good, it was only man that was out of harmony with it. I was inherently good, not evil as our Western society has taught me as a child; all people were intrinsically good. Neither time nor space existed on this plane. I saw into the past and observed man's endless struggle toward the light. Love and suffering and compassion for the whole human race so suffused me that I knew I never again could hate any person no matter what he did. I also saw into the distant future and beheld man awakening gradually to the good in himself, in others, moving with the harmonious rhythm of the universe, creating a new golden age — in some sweet tomorrow.

All the profoundest questions of life were answered, debilitating doubts dispelled, insoluble conflicts resolved. The unity of all things and all people became a deeply vivid, undeniable experience, the eternal verities a felt reality, opposites reconciled.

How long this blissful state lasted — a minute, an hour — I shall never know. Just as suddenly I returned to consciousness. I did not know where I was, what time of day it was. I felt disoriented as if I had been on a long trip to a distant strange country. The sight of my old desk and the blue couch was reassuring. But what on earth had happened to me? What did it all mean? Was I queer — or worse — losing my mind?

Had the vivid reliving of all the "small ecstasies" of my entire life precipitated this mysterious rebirth? Or was it the natural sequence that followed psychological death of the ego? I did not know — then.

At that time I never had heard of William James' psychological explanation of "dying to be truly born." I knew nothing of Carl Jung's psychotherapy and the "dissolution of the ego in the collective unconscious" at the universal level to attain self-realization, nor of Jean Houston's Integral level of the unconscious where the religious and mystical experience occurs. I had heard repeatedly as a child that Jesus said, "Unless you (die and) are born again you cannot see the kingdom of heaven." I had never met anyone who had the faintest conception of its meaning — nor had I — until now.

I was too ignorant to be aware that this kind of psychological **spontaneous** death and rebirth was the discovery of the self that had happened in far greater degrees in Whitman, Millay of *Renascence*, to Jung and Schweitzer, to Goethe and Dante, Beethoven and even Socrates and that afterward they produced their finest work.

I did not know that this kind of inner transformation is the goal of all the higher religions, especially Buddhism, Hinduism and Sufism, of Christian mysticism, and Hasidic Judaism, of Jung's psychotherapy, of the dialectic of Socrates (even though reason was his means) and even dancing of certain kinds. Like others of the Western world, I had been dominated too long by the rational conscious mind to believe that self-realization, enlightenment, satori, samadhi, is the most effective way to solve our basic problems of life. Our education does not teach us techniques for actualizing our finest potentialities. It does not teach us how to love our neighbors as ourselves, desire to serve others, peace and cessation of attachment to material things or the death of hate and jealousy and fear of death as does the attaining of the highest state of consciousness.

It was astounding to discover that cosmic consciousness transformed my life, my marriage, my character, behavior and values for twelve glorious years. I was unaware until later that self-realization awakened in man the certitude he is forever seeking, the courage he wishes he possessed, the creativity for which he longs. It evokes a selflessness of which he did not know himself capable, a love of the human race that astounds him, a sense of union with the life force his rational mind had assured him was impossible. It brings greater rapport with nature, a deeper response to the beauty of the arts and a joy exceeding all others. It even produces an embarrassing charisma.

The unenlightened are naturally skeptical of the incredible results of activating the deepest levels of the unconscious which are common to all men — until they too have experienced it. It is above and beyond intellectual comprehension. The actualization of human potentials means becoming what one already is. It is a discovery of one's true self.

"Bringing the eternal into the now" is the noblest endeavor possible to man. Enlightenment is more deeply satisfying than any of man's most cherished goals — wealth, power or fame, love, passion, beauty — or eternal youth.

Self actualization reveals the secret of human happiness, the goal of living, the meaning of life.

VACATION

My husband returned to Cape Cod in May, went house hunting till exhausted, finally late one night rushed through a small cottage and signed the lease.

When we arrived to take possession in June we found to our utter dismay — beds with springs 30 years old, blankets full of spots and frayed ends, tired old couches, wicker chairs which squeaked like mice all night long. No telephone, no door bells, no radio, no clocks; ah ha, this would cure my husband forever of his desire to return to the simple life. I prepared to suffer for three months like a silent martyr.

It was the most glorious summer of our entire lives. (In spite of our anxiety about America entering the Korean War. It was 1950.)

June and July sped by. Every morning we worked. I closed all the doors. He typed in the living room. I typed in my bedroom. My book was progressing — not steadily — but by leaps and bounds. There were virtually no interruptions. We avoided the neighbors. We wanted privacy.

Every afternoon we went swimming.

Immediately after breakfast every day my husband departed for the village to make his long-distance business calls and collect the mail. The summer colony all around us was asleep at this early hour.

Each morning I sat out on the flagstone terrace alone with the sea and blessed quiet, enjoying the warm comforting process of digestion, relaxing like a contented cat, hoping my day's writing would rise up from the dark night of the unconscious like a slow tide.

One morning everything was different. It felt as if Walt Whitman suddenly bade me "loaf and invite my soul"[1] — in prose dying to be poetry:

THE PERFECT DAY

I sit alone on the terrace overlooking the sea
On this first hot August day.
Gone are the months of cold and fog
And fickle Cape Cod wind.
"Sit still, sit still!" I say to myself,
"Let the sweet summer sun sink into you
Body and senses
Don't read, don't think, don't move."

Gradually like the unnamed fragrance of an unseen flower,
All the meaning of nature's summer,
All the meaning of the summer of my life, of my mature thinking,
Steals slowly through my sentient being,
And I say to myself: Look! Look at the sea!
Never was it so luxurious a blue
None of your pale anemic blues of faint-hearted June
None of your delicate aquamarines, nor milky green jades,
None of your steel grey sheets spread under a leaden sky
Nor the dark boiling roiling grey of a distant storm —
But blue, BLUE! Its rightful, royal blue,
Thank God, the sea has come into its own at last!

And the sky! Never was this pale puritanical sky
So bold and daring a blue!
Gone is the daily disappointment to hungry Southern eyes,
Born under the fabulous Texas sky of tropical blue.
And that one single white cloud
Boiling up on the horizon,
Was there ever a cloud so achingly, dazzlingly white!
The one beautiful blot on heaven's blue escutcheon.

And the sun, "the splendid silent sun" — [2]
Has it ever poured over my avid face,
Over the whole sun-hungry earth
In such a hot golden flood?
And the air — dear God, how sweet it is!

Cool and clear and dry.
No visible veil of grey fog.
But wait, wait! This is a day with a difference.
Why this distillation of all summer days in one?
Wind — ah yes — **there is none!**
Our daily undesired companion has vanished at last.
For this thrust of land — bathed, buffeted, by two fitful oceans —
This Cape of the Cod, can boast of the world's most variable wind,
Now its blessed absence bequeaths us
One of those rare vibrant days,
When the earth stands still and steeps in its own glory.
Today every tree, every bush before my eyes waits poised,
A study in arrested motion,
"A pause more dynamic than motion."[1]
No breeze singing its daily song
Through the homely little Cape Cod pines,
Only the spicy scent locked in the pine needles
Drawn out by this hot August sun
As love draws out nobility long dormant in a lover.

I hold my breath and listen — to the blessed **silence.**
The whole earth is caught in some magic stillness —
Not of death but vibrant with invisible life — waiting —
And the sea! what has happened to that incessant surf
Always splashing, spanking, sighing, sucking at the shore?
Every day for two months, any hour night or day
I could hear the plaint of the sea,
Incredulous, I turn an ear sideways and listen,
Not a sound! Even the mighty ocean has paused to rest.
Silence, surpassing all music, lays her sorcerer's spell over me,
Soothing every raw nerve end, every rioting emotion, every fractious
      thought.
Has the earth's heart stopped throbbing, too?
Or is she merely resting on her laurels,
Replete after work well done,
Summer being the promise of spring fulfilled.
Now all nature holds her breath waiting — for what?
I do not know.
I too hold my breath, waiting —
For the disclosure of Nature's deepest mystery perhaps?
Then suddenly the cicada!

CICADA

Suddenly summer's first cicada
Cleaves the silence in two like a swift arrow of sound
That long strident crescendo pierces me with strange delight,
Awake! the song of the cicada says, summer is already on the wane!
Soon winter will grey the ocean, pale the sun;
I am the herald of summer's approaching death.
Now is the high moment of nature's life, of your life,
The song of the cicada says,
Look long and lovingly,
For now the sea is a deeper blue,
The trees a lusher green, the sun a richer gold.
Store up, store up, all the sweet summer sights and sounds
To sustain you through the long winter of your discontent.
Lie down in the stream of summer and let it flow over you.
The time of anticipation is over,
The days of realization are come, the cicada says.

THE SIMPLE LIFE

But not in a day is wisdom born.
So August passes, summer is ending
Simple wisdom beginning.
And once again I sit on the terrace
Alone with the sea and sun
And I say to myself
And I say to you
Summer brings fulfillment to all the living earth
So let summer bring fulfillment to you,
To your body, mind, and spirit —
In that order,
Return to nature
Periodically if not permanently,
Return to the simple life
Live in a little cottage by the sea
Return to forgotten fundamentals
To basic unchanging values
To elemental wisdom.

Houses — leave them behind
Take your white body and prison-pallored thoughts
Walk out into the healing sun again;
Streets — with their hard soulless surfaces —
Scorn their touch, seek the soft friendly earth;

Shoes — the solitary cells in which we condemn our guiltless
    feet
Leave them behind like a pagan
Walk barefoot on the resilient seaside sand
Slowly — aware —
Planting each sensitive white foot, each slow leg, like a hungry
    tree taking root in the good earth;
Clothes — convention's cruelest cage —
Free the poor punished body,
Let it return like a wild bird to its natural habitat in the depths
    of summer;
Clocks — civilization's whip cutting so cruelly into our modern
    lives — leave them in the city;
Society, servants, neighbors — even friends —
Shun them, return to the sweet solace of solitude;
Noises — modern mechanical noises
Telephones, door bells, radios,
Escape from their little stinging blows
Return to the healing sounds of the sibilant sea,
The whispering wind, the singing birds;
Activity — reject it, neglect it.
Do nothing — glorious nothing
Let idleness lap about your agitated spirit
Like warm healing waters;
Walk out on mechanical materialism,
Do not be foolish. Do not reject all modern gadgets.
To do so, is to make of woman a household drudge,
Of man a primitive peasant;
Retain the minimum of modern conveniences
The ones you can master which will not master you.

If you are a woman, custom bound, and burdened as men never
    are
Forget your **perfume**, paint and perfect grooming,
Laugh at all the fickle changing fashions
In clothes, in politics, art, and ideas
Cast them aside like a constricting coat
Dive deep into the eternal verities
Come up laughing with seaweed in your hair
With shining visions in your eyes
Memories of the indescribable wonders of the
    undersea world
Where life's buried treasures lie.
How? But how?

RELAXATION

I say to myself
And I say to you
Free yourself of things and people
Plunge into the heart of nature
Then let go, let go,
Say with Huxley, "Let go body and soul,"
With Lawrence, "Live from the unconscious."
Relaxation is modern man's secret weapon
Against his invisible enemy — over-civilization.
So free yourself from tensions,
How? But how?

Lie still, lie still, on the soft sandy shore
Don't talk, don't look, don't think.
Let go, let go — feel — feel.
Welcome the weight of the hot heavy sun
As you gladly bear the weight of your beloved
And the sun, like a skillful lover, will pierce your flesh with its
        fertile kiss
Untangle your knotted nerves, unloose your tense
        muscles,
Sweeten your hostile emotions, crystalize your vague
        thoughts
Float your spirit away on the universal tide
And "your flesh shall be a great poem,"[3]
As Whitman said so long ago.
Swim naked in the great green sea
If you can, if you dare
Abandon yourself to its cold stinging embrace
It will awaken your body to new life
Cleanse you of folly and fatigue and fear,
Rest wet and naked, if you can, if you dare
On the solacing sands
Drink into your every hungry pore
The warm nourishment flowing from the breast
Of your eternal mother — the earth.

Let the **body** have its day for one whole wonderful summer
Let the poor body
Harnessed all winter
Reined in here, lashed to greater speed there
Like an unwilling horse
Let it go free for one glorious once

Like the wild lovely animal nature designed it to be,
Let your body rediscover its own spontaneous rhythms,
It will reward you a hundred times over.

Don't follow the routine of season or reason
Don't obey the dictates of duty
Do what you **want** to do, **when** you want to do it.
Eat when you're hungry, sleep when you're sleepy
Not by clock or custom or conscience
Eat the simple foods, fresh from earth and tree and vine
Foods full of the flavor of soil and sun and rain
Eat with slow awareness
And your sense of taste will leap into new life.
And your grateful body
Like the most indifferent bird on the most unconsidered bough
With the same delightful nonchalance
Will perform its other natural functions.

Your **work** — writing or whatever
Let it wait, let it lie, let it sleep,
Let it slowly rise like an undisturbed river
Deepening at the dam of the unconsciousness
Later to gush forth in a joyous flood
That will sweep you on to glory.
Your **desire** — let it wait —
Till it surges up like the waves of the sea
Clamoring to break into ecstatic climax.
Your daily **annoyances**, weekly disappointments
Your monthly pains
No, they will not disappear
But they cannot pierce through the soft warm cloak
     of utter relaxation.
Your **sleep** — it will come as never before
You will sink into the black fathomless well
Of sweet nothings
Back into the womb of time
Till you are born again each morning with the innocence of a child
Fresh with wonder and delight
At the world and everything in it
Especially yourself
And your unsuspected store of inner riches,

FULFILLMENT

So be yourself, your own true self
Be all your many selves
Even your natural animal self,
Free the body from its unnatural restraints
And it will not — paradoxically enough —
Reduce you to an animal existence
It will lift you to another higher plane.

Now your body — relaxed, renewed
Will quietly relinquish the major role in your life
Now your body, not you, will gently thrust into the background where
    they belong
All the daily necessities —
Bathing — brushing — dressing
Eating — sleeping —
Even housekeeping.
Now your body will move through the hours
With slow calm unsuspected efficiency
With the ease born only of relaxation
Not your master but your servant,
The ideal servant, effacing itself,
Performing its daily duties quietly — deftly,
Even achieving oblivion to weather and discomfort,
To hunger and fatigue — up to a point
Freeing your mind and then your spirit
In that order
Their works to perform.

Now your **thoughts** will consort
No longer with petty inconsequentials
But with the destiny of man
The problems of the world
The eternal verities.
Your mind like a swift white bird
Freed from the cage of bodily distractions
May be lifted on the wings of ecstasy
To realms of pure white truth
Soar to unknown heights
Bringing back rare materials
To build into a new poem
A broader philosophy
Or perhaps a more comprehensive religion?

And your **spirit** —

If only for one long summer
You mix and mingle with the spirit of the universe
Diffused in sun and sea and sand
If only for one sweet summer you immerse yourself in nature
Live the simple life
Relax to your uttermost depths,
Release your deepest truest self
Then in the summer of the year
And the summer of your life
You will learn that the mystic tides of the unknown
Will rush back in periodic ebb and flow
Cleansing you of fear and doubt
Washing away pettiness and hostility
Selfishness and injustice
Filling and feeding you to overflowing
With love of the whole human race
For you have learned at last
That you are good inherently
Therefore all men are good
Because we all partake of the same absolute good.
And finally you know that someday
Your spirit, like a river
Will flow into the great universal sea
Mix with it
Merge with it for time everlasting
For you know there is no death.

WISDOM

So look for the good in man
Where — but in yourself?
Look for the God in man
Where — but in yourself?
Look for the basic solution
To the world's basic problems
Where — but in the reestablishment
Of long lost contact
By man, the eternal child,
With his father, the universe
And his mother, the earth
In the sea and sun of summer.

For one warm expansive moment
When the deeper self is liberated
When the loving, ethical self

The intuitive, spiritual self
Is freed briefly from Reason —
That modern necessary prison —
Such an awakening can alter
Your entire bewildered life.

For one glowing transcendent moment
Can place in your hands the magic key
To the meaning of life,
For the secret of life
Of happiness and health
Of peace and security
And love of others
Is the achievement of union
By whatever means
However brief and inexplicable
However unreasonable and unscientific
With the great life force
The ceaseless mystery
Of the timeless universe.

(Or will Reason, dethroned, protest?)

PART IV

REASON

PREVIEW

What, our Reason demands sooner or later, *is* this ecstatic release of our deeper self, this sense of union with some higher power?

It is merely a **poetic** experience — faintly resembling that of Whitman or Millay, Wordsworth or Dante?

Or is it **philosophical?** Intuitive insight into the nature of things? Can Plato or Kant, Bergson or Emerson, or Northrop explain it? Can it be the teleology of tomorrow? The spiritual grounded in science as Edmund Sinnott and Ruth Anshen intimate?

Or is it **psychological?**
Is it neurotic as Freud claims?
Or the result of our type of physique as Sheldon implies?
The latest step in evolution according to Bucke?
Or is James correct, "The spirit of the universe is your own subconscious self"?
Or is ecstasy the spontaneous release of the deeper layers of our normal "collective unconscious," as Jung maintains?
And what of those born psychologists, the great writers?
Virginia Woolf believes it to be contact with an impersonal truth outside ourselves.
Aldous Huxley considers ecstasy a mystical experience inducible by a chemical change in our body's blood sugar.
Or is it **religious?**
Is this what Buddhism means by Nirvana?
Or Hinduism by union with Brahman?
Or Christianity by an "experience of God"?
Which one is correct?

CHAPTER 23

PSYCHOLOGISTS

RETURN

Then the most awful thing happened. A storm of doubt assailed me. Skepticism awakened me in the night like flashes of lightning. But I ran away from the voice of reason for a few days.

We packed up the car, left the hideous little old cottage and the most glorious summer of our lives behind us. We negotiated the seven-hour return drive to Connecticut as easily and unerringly as homing pigeons. With every mile, the old nameless causeless exuberance welled up inside me like a bubbling spring. I had not known its like since I was a young girl in lyric harmony with life.

Neighbors called to welcome us home. "You both look radiant, radiant!" they exclaimed.

The maids and the yardman rushed out to carry in the luggage. We were so glad to see them we could have hugged them. And in the days that followed we felt more grateful to them than ever before. They relieved us of those inexorable daily chores, freeing us for other work nearer our heart's desire. They had everything in the house shining within an inch of its life. The garden was a model of tidiness.

After three months' absence I walked about from room to room literally patting the walls. I gazed with fresh eyes at the Adam-green paneling, the long sweep of the red damask draperies, the crystal chandeliers that tinkled at every footstep.

Never had I loved my home so much, never had I felt so grateful to my husband for surrounding me with beauty. Never had we appreciated the spaciousness of our colonial house so keenly. Its dignity seemed to increase our dignity. Its graciousness seemed to lend us a little more graciousness toward the whole world.

Was anything so satisfying as civilized city life, we asked each other? Provided you could return periodically to nature, to the simple life. Variety was more than the spice of life. It was a necessity.

Soon I withdrew to my study on the third floor. Fondly I hoped this book would continue writing itself with the spontaneous flood of the summer. It didn't. A storm broke loose.

Reason, dethroned for the whole long exciting year by the flow of the unconscious, reasserted itself arrogantly. It rejected everything. My own reason.

What in the name of common sense do you think you've been doing this last year? my conscious mind demanded. Proving the existence of a God? Intuitive knowledge is not valid. Only reason can acquire that. Feeling is no royal road to wisdom. Only logic can point the way. Your fine ecstatic experiences prove nothing — except that you may be pathological!

This was terrifying. This was indeed a return — not only to our house but to the former tyranny of reason. Had I been living in a fool's paradise for a whole year? Had I been cured of my despair about man's evil nature only to find the cure worse than the malady?

How do you know there is some cosmic principle for men to unite with, my rational self asked? You don't. No one does. It is scientifically unverifiable. Science informs us man stands utterly alone on this spinning planet. The whole universe may be merely a self-started mechanism. This is the opinion of most intellectuals today, scientists, and philosophers. Who are you to feel differently? I refuse to accept any of your fine and fancy conclusions — unless you can verify them by science.

I couldn't.

Well, then, is there any rational explanation, reason insisted, of this joyous intuitive insight into the nature of things? In short, **what is ecstasy?** Or the mystical experience? Or the psychological release of our loving, ethical, esthetic, intuitive, deeper self?

Is it merely a poetic experience? Or psychological? Or philosophical? Or is it religious?

I did not know.

So I launched into intensive research. It was to continue for four exciting years. I rushed to the original sources. To the books of the profounder poets, psychologists, philosophers, and to the bibles of the world. I plunged into the deep waters of abstraction far over my poor layman's head. I was caught in the dangerous crosscurrents of contradictory opinions. I wrestled with the profoundest problems that engage the mind of man. The meaning of life, the nature of the self, the universe, and man's relation to it and to his fellowmen. The problems of the ideal society, of good and evil, death, immortality, and God. These questions stretched the unused muscles of my untrained mind to the breaking point.

FREUD

Would not Freud condemn such ecstatic experiences as neurotic, infantile, and sublimation of sexuality? Gathering all my courage together, I made the dangerous plunge into the icy waters of honesty. At first the shock was paralyzing, then a stimulating challenge to fight my way out.

I read and reread his books. They were too difficult for a layman. So I studied Freud under a Yale professor for an intensive year.

The unconscious which Freud had discovered was one of emotional disturbance originating in childhood before the age of six. It was full of neurotic guilt, conflict, unmotivated hostility toward others, depression, infantile repressions, a sense of rejection by parents or siblings, sexuality, love-hate fixation on mother or father, complexes, and inability to love anyone.

The spontaneous variety of ecstasy, however, was a flow from a source of joy, harmony, and fulfillment. Freud's psychology was for sick people, for neurotics. There must be another kind for glorious health. Surely this joyous kind of outpouring from the unconscious was not neurotic.

Was it infantile? Freud condemned all religion as an infantile dependence on a God as a father-mother substitute. But such happy experiences were no blind obedience to some irrational power, no immature helplessness, no submissive begging for personal favors.

Instead, the spontaneous release of this part of our unconscious mind, if that was what it really was, produced an awakening to the good, the true, and the beautiful long lain dormant in our deepest self. And more. It aroused unsuspected love of others. It brought a sense of communication with some ineffable good inherent in the structure of the universe. It increased our independence and strength. It did not make a person feel like a miserable sinner crawling in the dust of repentance. On the contrary, for one blinding moment a mere human seemed to partake briefly of godlike attributes.

Was it the sublimation of sexuality? That was a very broad term as Freud employed it. But it was true that certain kinds of intellectual ecstasy did seem to resemble the erotic, strangely enough. For example, last year when a scientist at Yale introduced me to Dr. William Sheldon's Constitutional Psychology, the reading of his books *Varieties of Physique* and *Varieties of Temperament* absolutely overwhelmed me.

One morning in my quiet study on the third floor of our house I had been reading *Temperament* for hours with steadily increasing excitement. This book answered questions I had been asking for years. Learning was absolutely a thrilling process. As truth after truth was unfolded before my astonished eyes, I felt deliriously happy.

Finally on page 276 one sentence pierced me with ecstasy. I closed my eyes, held my breath, my heart pounding like a drum while unbearably sweet rapture seemed to seize my body, mind, and emotions. Time ceased to exist...

Golden warmth flooded all my being. I drifted in a sea of perfect joy —

all questions answered forever — all doubts dispelled...

Surely the acquisition of logical truths could not be erotic, yet the mystics in monasteries and nunneries often wrote of the results of their meditations in erotic terms. Or was the involuntary release of any bodily tension similar because it involved the same autonomic nervous system? This was an avenue for investigation for scientists — not laymen. Thus a psychological, even spiritual, awakening might appear to be a sublimation of sexuality but it was far more than that.

Then the answer was that Freud undoubtedly was a genius. Ecstasy sometimes was neurotic in neurotic people. And doubtless some religious fanatics were neurotic. Many religious people might be infantile. But there seemed no proof that all religious people were neurotic or that all ecstatic release of the ethical, loving, esthetic, intuitive part of the human psyche was pathological.

I had observed several people who had undergone Freudian analysis turn automatically to religion. Undoubtedly the Freudians were necessary to bring greater health and happiness to suffering humanity but also to remove neurotic obstructions that might lie in the path to a great awakening of a deeper unconscious. Most of the neurotic persons I had studied were handicapped by the feeling of having been unwanted children not by any form of sexuality.

(Later I read in Dr. Ira Progoff's book, *The Death and Rebirth of Psychology* that in their old age, Freud, Alfred Adler, and Otto Rank all admitted that the psychologist must delve deeper than a man's neurosis into his normal healthy creative unconscious...)

But where was this psychology of the normal healthy man and the awakening of his deeper better self? What of Sheldon?

SHELDON

Varieties of Temperament answered hundreds of questions: why are men different? why are some kind, others cruel? some energetic and others indolent? and why could there never be one truth for all men? But did our type of physique and temperament also determine our ability or inability to experience the awakening of the intuitive part of our minds?

Sheldon presented scientific laboratory evidence that our type of physique determined our temperament. For twenty years he had measured and graded the physiques of some 4,000 people on a seven-point scale. He derived his terms for the three types of physiques from the three layers of cells which composed the human embryo: the endoderm, mesoderm, and ectoderm. These layers developed respectively into guts, etc; or bones and muscles, or nerves and skin, etc. But the proportions differed in different people's bodies and that made their temperaments different. There were actually seventy-six combinations but nearly all were dominated by one of the three constitutional components.

Sheldon classified a man's physique as endomorphic if his alimentary apparatus was predominant, or mesomorphic if his muscle and bone dominated the other components of his body; or ectomorphic when his skin was literally thinner and he had more nerve area exposed, and weaker muscles.

In temperament then Sheldon designated the round soft fat endomorphic body-build as having a viscerotonic temperament. That is, a person loving food, people, comfort, etc. The stocky broad strong-muscled large-boned mesomorphic physique produced a somatotonic temperament. That is, a temperament which liked action, liked to exercise, to dominate others, overcome obstacles, etc. The third was the slender ectomorphic physique with small bones, small stomach, and small intestinal tract which gave evidence of a cerebrotonic temperament. These were intense nervous high-strung persons who did not care too much for physical action, sports, food, or people but preferred solitude and displayed often a passion for knowledge.

Boldly I had asked Sheldon his somatotype. In physique he was tall and handsome and charming in manner, a 3-4-5 in endomorphy, mesomorphy, and ectomorphy respectively; and in temperament a 3-4-5 in viscerotonia, somatotonia, and cerebrotonia. When a man was a 5 in ectomorphy he often was a genius. Only God could be a 7-7-7, that is, "all-loving, omnipotent and omniscient."[1]

The 4-4-4 was the person as heavily endowed with each component as was humanly possible. Sheldon described this as "the supremely intelligent"[2] type in his early books. Later he changed it so radically it staggered me.

For Sheldon's woman assistant somatyped me. I was a 4-4-4.

If our physique determined so many things about us, the way we slept or didn't, the things we liked to eat, the diseases to which we were susceptible, our courage or cowardice, our philosophy of life — then surely our type of body-build must exert tremendous influence on our capacity or incapacity to experience the spontaneous ecstatic release of our deeper unconscious, didn't it? But how?

Varieties of Temperament said the extreme endomorph found his ecstasy in eating and comfort, the extreme mesomorph in overcoming obstacles, and the extreme ectomorph in "intensification of consciousness."[3] But what about the greatest of all ecstasies — man's union with the spirit of the universe? Not a word!

One day I took my courage in my hands and informed Sheldon I was writing a book on man's relation to the universe. Did he consider that important? "It's the most important thing in life," he replied.

He introduced me to his earliest book, *Psychology and the Promethean Will.* This book was stimulating and reassuring even to the most skeptical reason.

The Promethean will was man's urge to live to his fullest stature. Sheldon however did not agree with Freud and Jung about man's possession of an unconscious. He believed we had a higher and lower consciousness.

But Sheldon did agree with Jung that "The diagnosis of the modern sickness is — dissociation. At the more educated levels of life people have lost touch with their own souls. Stated in psychological language a general dissociation has come about in the human mind between the lower consciousness and higher consciousness."[4]

"When a meaning is emotionally felt the resulting awareness may be called a feeling of wholeness, a flash of insight or intuition; the aesthetic experience; and on rare occasions the mystic experience, or the intense experience of the soul. It is this experience of the soul which seems to constitute the final goal of all human striving. When it is achieved, man is at home in his universe."[5]

He also stated that after intense concentration, the intellect sometimes reaches a joyous climax of understanding similar to the supreme physical rapture, but gave no explanation.

The theme of this book was that the only hope for psychology in the future was a religious psychology and the only hope for traditional religion was a psychological religion. People who "maintain the heart of a child through life are very possibly our closest approach to the Christ ideal. [When] the curiosities and warm emotional imaginings of childhood...[become] combined with unusual intellectual maturity a great mind appears on the earth. It is the cardinal prerequisite of a great mind and more common in women than in men, there may lie an unsuspected source of hope in a human society which seems likely to be more influenced by women in the future."[6]

Sheldon classified the means through which man may achieve intuitive insight into the cosmic order: "People, things, creations, earth, and the universe."[7]

Why did he omit the most common one of all in mesomorphic America? The pleasure of the mesomorph in muscular motion — in dancing, swimming, and sports? That explained their popularity. And were there not more than five stimuli?

SEVEN STIMULI

Already my twenty beautiful experiences had fallen automatically into seven classifications according to the stimulus which precipitated them. Nature. The arts. Thought. Motion. Relaxation. Love and passion. The seven natural stimuli, or were there more?

Obviously no one could understand human nature properly until he understood how man's type of physique determined his type of temperament. Sheldon was a basic requirement for all thoughtful people — teachers, ministers, writers, doctors, psychologists, philosophers, and scientists, and all editors.

Sheldon discovered that the ectomorph was able to see within himself but that the mesomorph was almost incapable of understanding himself. Therefore if the latter did experience a religious conversion it was sudden and explosive.

Perhaps people like Buddha under the Bo tree and Paul on the road to Damascus felt it so overpoweringly that they remained on an exalted plane continuously the remainder of their lives. Much research might be conducted in this fascinating field by constitutional psychologists of the future. For apparently the frequency, number, variety, and intensity of a person's joyous direct apprehensions of the cosmic order depended primarily on his type of physique and temperament.

Sheldon contributed richly to the understanding of the self and of others but the search for a final answer must continue.

Was there some brilliant modern intellectual who **personally** had experienced this strange beautiful puzzling and rapturous awakening?

HUXLEY

One unforgettable day a tall distinguished English gentleman came to tea with me at my club in New York. Recently he had published a small book, *The Doors of Perception*. He quoted William Blake, the great mystic poet and painter, who said that if we kept our doors of perception always properly cleansed we could perceive the world as it really was — a holy place of beauty.

In this extraordinary little book, Huxley described his own amazing experiences after taking a more or less harmless drug, mescaline. It is employed in their religious ceremonies by certain American Indians to induce a proper sense of exaltation.

Aldous Huxley was the only intellectual I knew of who had displayed the courage to discuss the tabooed subject of mysticism in our modern age dedicated to Reason, Science, Politics, and Economics — the four gods of many men today.

For twenty years I had been reading the books of this brilliant Englishman — the bitter satiric novels and the essays. In the latter some wistful part of him seemed to be pursuing the will-o'-the-wisp of the mystical experience.

Preceding this meeting I had poured avidly again over fifteen volumes of his essays. Like an eager detective I searched for some personal reference between the impersonal lines.

For a lifetime, this wistful skeptic studied famous personages apparently in the hope of convincing himself that their apprehension of Ultimate Reality was valid. Of Pascal he wrote, "Being reasonable, Pascal disavowed rationalism and attached himself to revelation."[8] Of Spinoza, "The gist of all Spinoza's philosophy is that we ought to live and move and have our being in the infinite."[9]

The French philosopher, de Biran, Huxley said, seemed convinced that his whole mystical experience might be nothing more than a moment of bodily well being. The implication was that Huxley agreed.

This was disconcerting. Did not the physical well-being follow the ecstatic experience? It did not cause it. Or did it both preceded and follow? Only science could answer.

These three men were not only interested in philosophy but in religion. Were these two disciplines incompatible or inseparable? Huxley also wrote extensive comments on the mystical literature of Hinduism, Buddhism, and Christianity.

He praised the "systematic meditation" and "spiritual exercise" such as were used in Hinduism as superior to the spontaneous awakening. He apparently regarded the transcendence of the self and the merging with the impersonal power of the universe as mystical and religious rather than psychological. He was wiser and more erudite than I ever could hope to be. He seemed to be attracted to the religious philosophy called Vedanta.

I was tempted to follow in his footsteps. For after several years of research, I was beginning to feel desperate from too many contradictory opinions.

Must everyone who had these shining visitations forsake all worldly pleasure, wear a loin cloth and a begging bowl, sit and contemplate his navel?

Or must he walk up and down the land preaching some new kind of gospel? Was the recipient of these golden gifts under obligation to that — that **Thing** — to be a martyr or a saint or retire to a nunnery or monastery?

Such gifts were an embarrassment of riches. Like having three arms or twelve fingers. Was there no way to incorporate these beautiful findings into the everyday life — for example, of a wife and homemaker and writer?

What was going to become of me? What would be my belief in the end? After three years of research my brain was fagged, my eyes dim, my nerves strained to the snapping point. Why not cease my search for the best rational explanation of this profoundest of all human phenomena — the release of the deeper better self? Why not abandon myself to the broad river of one of the higher religions — Hinduism or Buddhism or Christianity? Why not allow these great emotional streams to carry me effortlessly along wherever they willed?

For the first twenty years of my life I had been immersed in the old-fashioned cruel fundamentalist religion of the Old Testament. At twenty-five, Reason cast all religions out the window because the problem of evil made them untenable. For twenty years I lived quite happily as an agnostic. Now in maturity was Reason itself beginning to realize that perhaps my conception of religion was erroneous, that it might be a glorious fulfillment, purification, and rebirth of all the buried good inherent in us all?

I lacked sufficient intellect, training, and education in spite of my three colleges to unravel all the complicated threads. Reason asserted that science was the only solid stepping stone to carry my uncertain feet safely across this rushing torrent of dangerous emotional currents which might sweep me off to who knows what fearful exotic fate. Reason saw nothing wrong with a worldly life. Why not the best of both worlds? Worldly and spiritual?

When Mr. Huxley walked into the drawing room at my club it was a relief to see how normal this famous mystic looked — beautiful tailored and perfectly groomed with admirably formal manners. After I served him tea, I made bold to ask him an extremely personal question. Had Sheldon ever somatotyped him?

Not in his laboratory. Sheldon **guessed** Huxley to be a 1-2-7 in viscerotonia, somatotonia, and cerebrotonia respectively. A 7! That was astounding. Surely indicative of genius.

"Do you think the very magnitude of your reason makes it difficult for you to relax sufficiently to release the unconscious?"

He smiled deprecatingly. "It might be."

"Have you ever experienced mystical ecstasy prior to taking mescaline?" I inquired.

"Only in a dim faint way."

The harmless drug, however, had brought him the "beatific vision"[10] such as William Blake and the poet AE had known. Colors vibrated glowingly as they must have done to the eyes of the great Dutch painters of still life. Folds of cloth took on the mystical power they evidently had possessed for the great Greek sculptors.

With others, Huxley investigated scientifically this phenomenon of awareness of the *mysterium tremendum* produced by mescaline. It worked on the central nervous system depriving the brain of its usual amount of glucose.

Did this prove that the process of realizing reality was nothing but a physiological state? In the natural method did not our emotions first cause the chemical change in the body? This in turn probably acted as the magic key which unlocked "the doors of perception."[11] The contents revealed in our unconscious were present all the time. It was only the problem of freeing them.

"Do you consider the mystical experiences produced artificially by a chemical as valid?" I inquired.

"Yes," Huxley replied.

After I returned home I reflected that as the grandson of the most famous exponent of Darwinism, Huxley should understand evolution as few moderns did. For he was one of the few intellectuals who synthesized science, art, religion, politics, and economics, and philosophy, though he had written very little on the variuos psychologies with the exception of Sheldon whom he admired greatly.

In one essay he had written, "Evolution can continue to be a genuine process only when. . .all the organism [advances] along the whole biological front and not with one part of itself or in one particular direction only."[12]

Could this possibly mean that the eventual aim of the evolution of the human species was toward a constitutional type in which all three components were equal? In some glorious tomorrow would man become equally loving, active, and full of knowledge — that is, equally endomorphic, mesomorphic, and ectomorphic? What **was** the ultimate goal of evolution — if not godlike man?

This might increase individual happiness and world peace. But what of the geniuses? The extreme types like Huxley, Sheldon, and Jung and Freud? Certainly they contributed more to civilization than the present 4-4-4's like myself.

Or were contributions made on two planes? One on the rational plane and the other on the spiritual, ethical, poetic, and artistic?

The Hindu philosophy of Vedanta which Huxley followed was remarkably similar to the spontaneous form of awakening. But where was there a modern scientific explanation for Western man?

JAMES

But were not spontaneous spiritual phenomena visited only on great religious leaders like Buddha, Jesus, and Krishna; on saints like Saint Teresa and Saint Augustine; or on religious fanatics?

William James in his *Varieties of Religious Experience* quoted many letters from other perfectly nice normal modern Americans. They too had "seen a light,"[13] felt a "presence,"[14] and undergone a sense of glorious union with some ultimate mystery. They proved that a person was not doomed to be a saint or martyr or a fanatic merely because he or she had been visited by such ecstatic moments. It might be a mark of normality and extreme good fortune according to the great Harvard philosopher and psychologist.

But why did ecstasy sometimes appear in fanatics and bigots? James did not elucidate that. Was it not because they were **already** extreme neurotics? But he did distinguish between the two varieties of ecstasy. The pathological variety which lead to morbidity, religious fanaticism, intolerance, and persecution of dissenters. And the other normal kind of ecstasy which lead to health, harmony with yourself, people, and the universe, and also prompted to ethical action. By their fruits you shall know them.

But surely James was wrong on one point. "The twice-born look down upon the rectilinear consciousness of life of the once-born as being 'mere morality'[15] ...The outlook upon life of the twice-born — holding as it does more of the element of evil in solution — is the wider and completer"[16]...The completest religions seem to be those in which the pessimistic elements are best developed...Buddhism and Christianity are religions of deliverance: the man must die to an unreal life before he can be born into the real life."[17]

"The healthy-minded, who need to be born only once, and the sick souls, who must be twice-born in order to be happy."[18]

Sick? No, no, for this would mean Christianity and Buddhism were sick. The sick souls were those who lived from reason alone, from the conscious mind only and suppressed their unconscious too long — like today's would-be intellectuals, including this one.

But I could take no credit for my rebirth. I merely allowed nature her wonders to perform. Why do we moderns refuse to listen to the voice of nature? We have nothing to lose but our despair.

"Saint Augustine, Saint Francis, Rousseau owed their influence to their feeling that Nature, if you will only trust her sufficiently, is absolutely good...[19] [then] a new zest adds itself to life, and takes the form of lyrical enchantment[20]...There is an unseen order and our supreme good lies in harmoniously adjusting ourselves thereto."[21]

This, however, is not so easy as it seems. James admitted, "My own constitution shuts me out from [the] enjoyment [of mystical states] almost entirely."[22] But why should brilliant talented men like James be incapable of spontaneous ecstasy when an ordinary woman could have some twenty experiences? What determined our capacity or incapacity to experience the involuntary release of our deeper unconscious? Was it environment or the type of stimuli or the type of individual?

BUCKE

Now came a contradiction of the psychological theory of James. Richard Bucke, a Canadian psychologist and biologist, claimed "cosmic consciousness" was the latest stage in the biological evolution of the race not a release of our own subconscious at all. He claimed it appeared only in a certain type of individual.

The lower animals, he stated, possess simple consciousness only, not self-consciousness. Human beings have evolved to self-consciousness. But even today it does not appear until a child is about three years old. Nowadays the third form of consciousness being added to the race is "cosmic consciousness," Bucke believed.

New faculties, he explained, are added to the human race not universally and simultaneously but individually and sporadically. Today some people are still color-blind and tone-deaf though the majority are endowed with the color and music senses.

Bucke's psychogenesis chart indicated that the color sense in man is approximately only 30,000 years old, the moral sense 10,000; the musical sense less than 5,000; and the cosmic sense "just dawning now,"[23] meaning in the last few thousand years. Someday all people will possess it.

He enumerated fifty cases of the cosmic sense: Buddha, Jesus, Paul, Mohammed, Dante, Blake, Whitman. Other examples were men of only partial cosmic consciousness: Socrates, Pascal, Spinoza, Wordsworth, Emerson, Tennyson.

He listed the sensation common to all men at the moment of this cosmic consciousness: a sense of presence, fear of going insane, awe, and joy. He enumerated as "the marks of the cosmic sense: subjective light, moral elevation, intellectual illumination, sense of immortality, loss of fear of death, loss of sense of sin, suddenness of awakening, added charm,"[24] etc. That list relieved my mind immeasurably. Ecstasy especially loves company.

Bucke even compiled a chart giving the age at which people had been visited by their greatest illumination. Buddha was 35, Jesus 35, Paul 35, Dante 35, Whitman 34, Mde. Guyon 33, Pascal 31. Apparently 35 was the magic age. Well, wasn't I thirty-five when I was writing my second book and that river of light descended into my own bursting little brain?

I hastened to compile an age chart of my own experiences. Undoubtedly age did determine which experience came at specific times. But developmental psychology was Arnold Gesell's field. He had discovered age to be a strong factor in the behavior of children but his research had not yet been extended to adults. A fascinating gold mine for future psychologists.

Bucke studied the physique and temperament of famous men with the cosmic sense and their parents as far as possible. He reverted to Hippocrates' classification of people according to their body "humours" which determined their temperament as choleric, sanguine, melancholic, or phlegmatic. He believed that the men with the cosmic sense possessed all four of these components in almost equal measure and therefore were destined for illumination.

But had not a more modern and scientific method of classifying physical and temperamental types been discovered by Sheldon?

What was the rational explanation of the release of the intuitive, ethical, loving, deeper self? **Freud** did not understand it. **Sheldon** implied it was constitutional. **Huxley** said it might be physiological. **James** thought it psychological. **Bucke** considered it evolutional. Who was correct? Were any of these answers complete? Was there no scientist who had conducted thorough research in this subject so vital to the happiness and peace of man?

JUNG

Did the analytical psychology of Dr. Carl Jung offer a rational scientific explanation of the release — spontaneous or induced — of man's ethical, intuitive, creative, deeper self?

Night and day, month after month, I poured over every book by Jung available in English.

Finally to clarify certain obscure points, I interviewed the grand old man of Switzerland in his home in Küestnacht. I wrote up the interview and published it in Paris.

So complicated a system as Jung's analytical psychology cannot be reduced to simple terms. But with all the temerity of a layman, I should summarize it thus:

The human psyche, or mind, according to Jung, is composed of four parts. The conscious mind — the place of Reason and Logic. The "personal unconscious" — home of the neurosis — if any. The deeper layers of what he calls the "collective unconscious" because it is the collected heritage from our ancestors throughout the centuries. And the Ego — of which we are all only too well aware.

Freud's great discovery was the personal unconscious and its neuroses and free association. Jung's great discovery was the healthy normal collective unconscious, of vital importance because it is the dwelling place of our moral, spiritual, esthetic, intuitive self. And the loving self, I believe.

Jung seems to think the sickness of the modern world — personal and political with its Fascism, Nazism, and Communism — can be attributed to the dissociation of man's conscious mind from his collective unconscious. Jung's therapy unites these two parts as nature intended to create the whole man. For centuries Western man — though not Eastern man — has lived primarily from his conscious mind worshipping Reason and its brilliant offspring, Science, to the exclusion of the inner man. Might this not explain the sad dilemma of many misguided modern intellectuals?

Jungian analytical psychology includes therapy for neuroses caused by present as well as past circumstances. But his greatest contribution is to normal psychology. He informed me that for fifty years hundreds of people had come to him from all over the earth — a third of whom were normal but unhappy because life seemed meaningless.

His therapy consists of discussion of problems — neurotic or otherwise, present or past — bringing unconscious material up into consciousness, and interpretation of dreams (these steps are painful), the drawing of mandalas — symbolical representations arising from the person's collective unconscious, and recognition of the archetypes, the old wise men, the earth mother, the shadow, the *persona*, and the *anima*.

Jung does not employ the terminology "the five steps" which I use but they are all present in his texts if the reader excavates long enough and deep enough: Suffering, "Death," Rebirth, Reason, and Wholeness.

Suffering: In all cases, normal or neurotic, some form of suffering precedes the seeking of assistance from a psychologist. And the person continues to suffer during analysis up to the turning point. There is a sense of abandonment to mysterious inner forces stronger than the individual's willpower.

"Death": Next comes a sense of dying caused by "the dissolution of the ego in the unconscious, a state resembling death."[25] If it feels like drowning in the sea that is due to the fact that "the sea always signifies the unconscious."[26] Naturally "death" in any form is painful. "The psyche is a self-regulating system. There is no equilibrium and no self-regulating system without opposition."[27] Therefore out of suffering comes joy, out of evil comes good, as the biblical psychologists discovered long ago. Struggling with the problem of evil apparently is as essential to man's mental growth as physical struggle for survival is to bodily evolution. When a scientist created an ideal environment for paramecia, they died. Struggle was not necessary to gain food or preserve life.

Rebirth: Evidently when human nature reaches the limit of its endurance, old mother nature takes charge. Then a mysterious law of psychology goes into operation: " 'enantiodromia' — the reversal into the opposite,"[28] Jung terms it. "Death" reverses itself into a sense of rebirth at the release of the collective unconscious as the good, the religious, the moral, and intuitive part of the psyche emerges. This brings joyous freedom though usually not ecstasy.

Reason: Next the conscious mind, having been held in abeyance, finally must understand and accept the irrational contents of the collective unconscious.

Wholeness: The process ends when these two separate parts of man's mind unite and he becomes whole. For the man of Reason is only half a man. The man of Intuition and Feeling is only half a man. Only the whole man can create the good life for the individual and the good society for all in a materialistic, physical, competitive environment.

"Nature," Jung said to me, "does not demand perfection of man but it does demand wholeness." And this entire process of awakening to the good in the self and wholeness he terms "self-realization" or "individuation."

According to his pupil, Jacobi, in *The Psychology of Jung*, "Jung leads the patient to an experience of God in his own breast."[29] Jung admits that the liberation of the collective unconscious is "a religious experience but no proof of the existence of a God."[30]

Many critics accuse him of being too mystical for a scientist. But he maintains that "it is precisely this 'mystical' idea which is...the natural tendency of the unconscious mind[31]...It is the mighty spiritual inheritance...born in every individual constitution...Morality is a function of the human soul."[32]

Jung's severest critics, the Freudians, often reject his basic premise. They assert that according to the principle of evolution the acquired characteristics of our ancestors cannot be inherited. Yet according to the facts of his observation of actual people — not a mere preconceived theory — Jung discovered that in its genetic development the collective unconscious of modern man repeats the religious experiences of the entire human race — even of the most primitive tribes — exactly as the human embryo passes physically through all the stages of evolution of the race.

These earlier forms reappear in men's dreams and the mandalas they draw or paint. In fifty years of research Jung has covered alchemy, myths, primitive religions, religious symbolism, religious systems, fairy tales — all deriving from man's collective unconscious otherwise they are unintelligible and incredible. He is now investigating extra-sensory perception. He has classified man into two types — introverts and extraverts but frankly it seems to me Sheldon's system of constitutional types is more advanced.

Jung warns us that the religious urge is as basic a drive as sex (Freud) or the will-to-power (Adler). "The idea of God...is a matter of tremendous energy and if man pronounces (him dead) the result will be a psychological disturbance in the form of dissociation of personality[33]...The educated public, the flower of our actual civilization, has lifted itself from its roots and is about to lose its connection with the earth."[34]

"If dull people lose the idea of God nothing happens — not immediately and personally at least. But socially the masses begin to breed mental epidemics of which we have now a fair number...If man declares the 'tremendum' is dead — it might appear under another name...something ending with — ism...of which people expect as much as they formerly did of God."[35]

Did not that explain the fanatical dedication of millions of people to Naziism and Communism?

"There is no question of believing but of experience. Religious experience is absolute. It is indisputable. You can only say that you have never had such an experience. No matter what the world thinks about religious experience, one who has had it possesses the treasure that has provided him with the source of life, meaning and beauty, and that has given new splendor to the world and to mankind."[36]

The reason dreams require interpretation by the Freudians and Jungians is because our unconscious — personal and collective — both speak — not in words — but in symbols and images. For the same reason Jung is obliged to help his patients interpret the symbols in their mandalas.

When a person in an exalted state seems to see a mountain or black clouds being rent asunder or a vast river of light, she is merely projecting in outward images the contents of her collective unconscious. Often the conscious mind is sufficiently alert even at the time to recognize them as subjective, not real.

And the reason a person in a moment of ecstasy becomes oblivious of her body, and her surroundings, of time and space is a quite reasonable scientific one. The collective unconscious does not register either time or space — only the conscious mind has achieved that. Thus a sensation of timelessness and spaceless infinity is not pathological but natural and normal for that older portion of the human mind.

What about light? — that sensation of blinding dazzling light which invariably accompanies man's most rapturous experiences? No one explains that — not James or Bucke or Huxley or even Jung.

What of the sense of union with a greater power than one's self? James says it is union with one's own higher consciousness. Jung as a scientist doubtless could not commit himself to man's awakening to the good in the universe or to the good in others as he had not observed those phenomena but only the individual's awakening to the good in himself.

Jung made what appeared at first an amazing statement, "to be 'normal' is the ideal [aim] for the unsuccessful. But for people of more than average ability, who never found it difficult to gain successes — for them to be [nothing but] normal signifies...sterility and hopelessness."[37]

So that was why a woman with a nice husband, a happy marriage, beautiful home, servants, enough money, pleasant social life, and modest success in her profession — one who "had everything" according to her friends could fall into despair. It always seemed so ungrateful, so unreasonable — until now.

What about wholeness? A pupil of Jung's, Dr. Esther Harding, leader of the Jungian school in America, states in *Psychic Energy* that "in ecstasy the individual loses his personal self and merges into something beyond himself. He does not feel this to be a loss, but a gain — he [is] renewed, made whole."[38]

Only temporarily was he not? Some extremely mesomorphic types might be visited by one such experience of merging which was so powerful that it lasted a lifetime.

But to a 4-4-4 type, for example, each momentary union with something greater was temporary. How could a person make it permanent — this sense of wholeness?

Jung supplied the answer to that difficult question also. The process of self-realization or individuation continued all one's life but the final climax came when the conscious mind accepted the contents of the collective unconscious usually in middle age.

Well, I was middle age now. It was of course a tremendous relief to learn that my despair, "death" and rebirth were merely natural laws of a normal mind. But my obstinate Reason was unable to unite with my unconscious even though it accepted Jung's explanation. Would I never attain it? Must I do more research?

Perhaps the time now had come to determine the real stimulus which had precipitated such ecstatic feelings as mine.

Motion: In "Wind," "Moonlight," and "Sea and Sand," muscular motion was the primary stimulus to awakening. Nature only ran a close second. This proved that the rhythmic movement of our own muscles — if mesomorphic enough — could open the locked doors and bring us spiritual perceptions, even a sense of immortality. This would explain the whirling Dervishes, the religious dances of American Indians, and of many primitive races.

Nature: In "Flowers," "Sun and Earth," and "Winter," nature was the primary stimulus. But why do the beauties of nature awaken us? Surely it is because the natural world is the visible manifestation of the eternal mystery. Can nature alone arouse us to timeless illumination? Doubtless, but in my case, love seemed to play a role in each instance. But so did relaxation.

Now I understood why D. H. Lawrence said that the scent of the flowers was a direct message from the source of creation.

Man believed in pre-existence, in a state of purity before birth not because he planned to, or wished to, but because it was a natural outpouring of the collective unconscious of the race.

Thought: In "Thinking" and "Thought," it was thought alone which acted as the precipitating factor. How paradoxical that our conscious thought — if prolonged and intense enough — can arouse our unconscious with all its strange treasures. That must be the secret of religious meditation.

But why the sensation of external sights? Of "seeing" a devil in a red suit when I was fourteen; of climbing a great mountain and "seeing" the black clouds roll back the night the millionaire gave me the elaborate dull dinner party?

"It is one of the peculiarities of invasions from the subconscious region to take on objective appearances, and to suggest an external control. The control is felt as **higher** since it is the higher faculties of our own hidden mind which are controlling, the sense of union with the power beyond us is literally true,"[39] James informs us.

No, Mr. James, the only sense of union I have felt so far was not with my own deeper unconscious but through the awakening of it, I felt a sense of union with a vast impersonal power in the universe infinitely superior even to the best in my own deeper mind.

The Arts: In "Painting," "Music," "Sculpture," "Architecture," and "Poetry" it was primarily the beauty of the art which awakened that sense of purification Aristotle says is the primary function of art. This leads to love of others, desire to serve, and a sense of union with some great creative principle in the cosmos.

In "Poetry," however, intense thought about the whole god-idea was a secondary influence. Poetry also brought intuitive insight into the nature of the universe.

In "Writing," it was not the beauty of someone else's art but the creative process itself which produced the river of light.

In "Drama," I really don't understand why I loved everybody. You tell me!

So at last I had fathomed the secret of the greatness of great art which had puzzled me all my life. Great art not only brought us a feeling of unity, and completeness, of stimulation and relaxation, refreshment and delight, order and harmony. Art was an avenue through which we could communicate with the eternal principle of the universe. Malreaux claims that traditional art celebrates the Absolute, modern art celebrates man only.

Love and Passion: Modern woman may love without passion, she may know passion without love, alas. But she is more likely to attain the heights where she sees the face of the unseeable when she both loves and is loved in the secure framework of marriage.

It is to laugh to see how wrong the Puritans were. How wrong all the haranguing Christian ministers of my Southern childhood were when they warned us against the body. For passion is the quickest and surest path to spiritual bliss — quicker than love, alas. Yet how logical that the act designed to create new life should be so closely allied with the great mystery of life itself. Do Puritan ministers really understand human psychology?

In his essay on D. H. Lawrence, Huxley writes, "And God the Father, the Inscrutable, the Unknowable, we know in the flesh, in woman."[40] So men achieved spiritual ecstasy through passion the same as women.

Relaxation: In "Summer" at Cape Cod the prolonged rapture was due primarily to relaxation but also to the simple life, swimming, and age — that is, maturity; added to the beauties of sea and sun and sky; added to love and marriage; and to thought; and creative writing. The work on my book flowed with delicious ease that summer. All these seven stimuli combined brought that year of "remembrance of things past," of reliving past incidents, to a glorious climax.

Our spontaneous awakening to the good in the self, in others, and in the universe could be stimulated by several natural means: nature, the arts, muscular motion, love, passion, thought and relaxation.

Which of the psychologists was correct in their analysis of these phenomena? Certainly each made indispensable contributions. But did any one of them cover the entire man?

Freud, I believe, was absolutely wrong that every ecstatic experience of this kind was neurotic. If a person were already abnormal it would be abnormal.

But Freudian analysis was essential in removing neurotic obstruction which might render progress along the path to the collective unconscious difficult.

Sheldon in his constitutional psychology certainly indicated that our type of physique and temperament determined many of our capacities and limitations. Therefore it was logical to assume that our somatotype might influence the spontaneousness, frequency, number, variety and the value of the results of the release of our deeper unconscious.

Huxley was undoubtedly correct that science revealed a change in body chemistry in all mystical states. In spontaneous cases, however, was it not the emotions which caused the diminution of glucose in the brain which in turn produced illumination? Both states could be produced by chemicals, breath control, fasting, asceticism, and meditation.

James cast much needed light on the varieties of religious experiences. But was he correct when he maintained that "the spirit of the universe is your own subconscious self"? Surely the lesser was only a part of the greater. To say they were identical was to make man include the universe. Or was it? If "seeing" a light and a presence, or hearing voices or seeing visions were all merely natural projections of a person's collective unconscious inherited from the race through the centuries, did not inexorable logic deduce that the report of an external supreme power was also subjective? Terrifying thought!

Here Reason itself leapt to the defense. How could any reasoning person look at the stars suspended in space, the rising and setting sun, the rhythmic tides of the sea, the incredible growth of a blue morning glory from a small brainless wordless black seed and at human birth itself, and believe the entire mystery of creation was contained in man. If logic meant anything, it reported that there must be a supreme power directing the cosmic system. But our most unshakable conviction derived from our collective unconscious.

Bucke studied only the spontaneous examples of "cosmic consciousness" in his fifty famous men. He omitted the innumerable cases where it was induced in Christianity and the Orient. Did he not err in explaining the cosmic sense as a third form of consciousness nature was adding to man? For Jung proved that all men possess a collective unconscious whence spiritual experience may arise. Bucke seemed correct that spontaneous awareness of the cosmic principle may be a product of evolution and only in persons approximating the 4-4-4 somatotype. In other types it appears to be potential.

Jung of course had conducted research in the liberation of man's deeper self more thoroughly than any of the other psychologists, professional or literary. His discovery that it was the awakening of the collective unconscious seemed indisputably logical. Certainly his record of the stages through which his patients passed to achieve "self-realization" when aided by his therapy was convincing beyond a doubt. His discoveries might lead the world toward great peace if properly employed and properly understood.

When I bade Jung goodbye after our memorable interview, I informed him I was writing a book about my own great awakening, the spontaneous release of my intuitive, ethical, loving, esthetic, spiritual self. But what if my book and my ecstatic rebirth were not accepted? How could I endure it? The grand old man looked me fiercely in the eye and said:

"Tell the truth and take the consequences. That's what I have been doing all my life. Expect to be misunderstood. People fear truth!"

And the truth was at this point that **I still did not feel whole.** My gratitude to Jung was inexpressible, my admiration unbounded. I considered his one of the greatest minds of this century. My Reason accepted his explanation of the psychological laws governing the release of man's collective unconscious, whether involuntary or evoked. His analysis of what I termed the "five steps" in the creation of the whole man: Suffering (or Despair), "Death," Rebirth, Reason, and Wholeness seemed incontrovertible. Personally however I did not **feel** whole. My conscious mind and collective unconscious existed as separate entities, no longer inimical but not united. Why had I failed so far to achieve that final wonderful sense of wholeness?

Must all the different strands of the different psychologies first be woven together into some meaningful pattern? My conclusion was that all the psychologists were correct as far as they went with only a few actual contradictions. No one system or concept covered the entire man, therefore a synthesis was necessary of all the psychologists: Freud, Jung, Sheldon, Bucke, Huxley, James, and Gesell.

Bucke's discoveries, however, seemed to point to a superior type of man in some distant tomorrow when man might evolve into a 5-5-5 somatotype. That is, a man who would be equally as eager for knowledge (ectomorphic) and full of feeling (endomorphic) as he already was active and powerful (mesomorphic) as witness his wars, bombs, planes, and ballistic missiles, wealth and comfort.

Then might not the prevalence of 5-5-5s mean spontaneous release of man's collective unconscious, the awakening of his intuitive, ethical, esthetic, loving, spiritual and peaceful self?

For what was the ultimate aim of evolution if not godlike man?

But before nature permitted me to experience completeness, must I test these psychological theories briefly at least against other disciplines — philosophy, religion, and the art of the profounder poets?

CHAPTER 24

POETS

WHITMAN

Now a brilliant new light illuminated certain difficult poets. I reexamined *Leaves of Grass*. Frankly I never had liked Walt Whitman. His euphoria had seemed to me excessive, his love of people and nature exaggerated, his interminable cataloging of things wearisome. Never had I found critics who made him clear to me either. They spoke only of his democracy, never of its origin, of his glorification or work and the "common man."

Now suddenly I saw there was an excellent reason for the warm glow that shone behind his every line. He had experienced a glorious release of his deeper unconscious. At thirty-four he had undergone his great awakening. Bucke, his doctor and friend, believed the poet had remained permanently on this high plane!

To Whitman it was sufficient merely to see, to catalog, a leaf of grass or a human being, to love it, to expand with his own goodness. To him all things and all people were but earthly symbols of an unearthly good pervading the universe. To his penetrating eyes, a serene light shone through them all. To him democracy was no political theory. Love of our fellows flowed from the release of our own better selves.

The ubiquitous "I" in Whitman was the universal "I." He was writing not of himself but of basic man, or as man might be tomorrow.

"He sees eternity in men and women."[2]

"Lo, the soul, above all science...
For it the mystic evolution,

Not the right only justified, what we call evil also justified."[3]

"Passage indeed O soul to primal thought...
Back, back to wisdom's birth, to innocent intuitions...
Fearless for unknown shores on waves of ecstasy to sail."[4]

MILLAY

I took down Edna St. Vincent Millay's "Renascence" from the shelf. This beautiful poem had delighted me when it appeared years ago. But with all the insufferable ignorance of youth I had dismissed her experiences as nothing but pretty poetic license — as did the critics. Suddenly today I saw that her sensation of death and burial under six feet of earth and final rebirth, her suffering the pains of all suffering humanity were but outward projections of actual inner mental and emotional experiences. I knew this because I had been drowned in the sea and reborn.

"And so beneath the weight lay I
And suffered death, but could not die.[5]

"Wind...thrust
Into my face a miracle
Of orchard-breath, and with the smell, —
I breathed my soul back into me.[6]

"The Universe, cleft to the core,
Lay open to my probing sense.[7]

"All sin was of my sinning
...Mine was the weight
Of every brooded wrong
[I] perished with each, — then mourned for all!...
A thousand screams the heavens smote;
And every scream tore through my throat."[8]*

(Had not I too felt the sorrows of the whole world?)

WORDSWORTH

Already he had come to my rescue in Alabama. He had seen children "trailing clouds of glory."[9] He had intimations of immortality and pre-existence.[10] And certainly the great Wordsworth was not pathological.

*From *Renascence and Other Poems*, Harper & Brothers, Copyright © 1912, 1940 by Edna St. Vincent Millay.

DANTE

Next I plunged into the *Divine Comedy*. I had not opened this book since I was a school girl. The best efforts of the professors to explain its deeper significance showed nothing but a mediaeval theological Catholic poem to my purblind eyes. Now on rereading it, I felt swept away on a fresh spring tide of joy and meaning. This was a psychological autobiography, a spiritual journey.

Dante had left the everyday world and journeyed into a strange psychological and spiritual world. He had been guided only so far first by philosophy, or reason, symbolized by Virgil and then by orthodox religion symbolized by Beatrice. Only when alone did he come face to face with the blinding radiance of the creative principle of the universe:

"So, round about me, fulminating streams
Of living radiance play'd...'[11]

"Light intellectual, replete with love;
Love of true happiness, replete with joy;
Joy, that transcends all sweetness of delight."[12]

"...I look'd
And, in the likeness of a river, saw
Light flowing[13]...

There is in Heaven a light, whose goodly shine
Makes the Creator visible to all."[14]

CHAPTER 25

BIBLES

CHRISTIAN

For years my high and mighty intellect in its abysmal ignorance had dismissed as scientifically untenable all the sacred writings of the world. The Vedas, The Upanishads, the Analects, also the Jewish-Christian Bible, and all the mythologies of all countries and all ages. The dogmas, rituals, allegories, and theological superstructure had obscured their underlying psychological foundations from me.

Today the prosecutor in this case, my own obstinate reason, finally was stunned into silence as old testimony was presented in the light of modern psychology and my own experiences.

Now old, trite, meaningless phrases from the Bible of my childhood leapt out at me vibrant with new life. "The Kingdom of God is within you."[1] In psychological terms this meant that the order of the cosmos was reflected in your own subconscious mind if you could but open that locked door. "Except ye become as little children ye shall not enter the kingdom of heaven"[2] meaning, not until the inborn goodness, the purity, buried in your own unconscious was released could you have a foretaste of immortality.

"Except a man be born again, he cannot see the kingdom of God."[3] Now that was not quite true. In all my greatest ecstasies I had "seen God" and yet I was not reborn until middle age. As I saw it, one was temporary. You died and were reborn only when you suppressed the religious urge in your subconscious too long. "God is love." Now I understood. Your deeper unconscious contained love and through aroused love you made contact with an illimitable source of love.

"For he who loseth his life shall find it."[4] The men of the Bible understood this kind of psychology centuries ago. I had indeed lost my life to find it!

In the light of psychology I now reinterpreted and clarified certain allegorical and Biblical concepts which had puzzled me all my life. Heaven, the fall of man, the garden of Eden. Also immortality and the soul. Did not all these ideas arise from men's actual experience with their own subconscious minds? Did not I, that day in Alabama, see with the mind's eye something innately pure in all children which might be called spirit or soul? Did not my own involuntary experience with locust flowers convince me of our preexistence in some idyllic state which some men termed a heaven? I had no conscious wish to believe these things. Reason resisted them. They merely flowed out of my own unconscious.

Could the "fall of man" mean that point in evolution when man's conscious mind was first added to his much older racial unconscious mind and reason or "eating of the tree of knowledge" first appeared? Had he until then been living from his unconscious with the blissful innocence of a child? Could the Garden of Eden represent that happy relaxed state when man was directed solely by his own healthy normal deepest subconscious which afforded him rapport with nature, with other human beings, and with the creative principle of life? Were the realistic scientists completely blind to poetic and psychological allegory?

And yet no, no! Did not Aristotle and Aquinas maintain that through reason man could know God? Well, certainly if you watched a small inanimate, brainless black seed grow into a tall blue morning glory, if you beheld the stars suspended in space, or observed the rhythm of the ocean, it seemed illogical **not** to believe in some kind of supreme power. Was this what Aristotle meant when he said the Unmoved Mover could be known through rational methods and that all things were drawn toward God? Or could Ultimate Reality be known both intuitively and rationally?

Why must men forever insist on everything being "either-or"? Why not "and?" Why not Reason **and** Intuition?

ORIENTAL

Now suddenly I saw that the magic key to the inner secrets of the great religions and religious philosophies of the ages lay within the grasp of anyone who had experienced a release of the collective unconscious. I began to study briefly Buddhism, Hinduism, Vedanta, Confucianism, Taoism, and Islam. But this was research for a lifetime.

How could I have been so stupid all my life? For now it was obvious that whatever their later accretions, most of them originally sprang from the same psychological root as my cosmic experiences, from man's apprehension of Ultimate Reality and a sense of union with it. Often it led to more ethical social behavior either passive or active.

But why did Buddha assert that "life was sorrow"? Why were most of these religions or religious philosophies pessimistic? Even Christianity was, wasn't it? Why did most of them dwell primarily on the life after death rather than the joy of life on earth?

Wasn't the human race today ready and eager for a radiant joyous philosophy or psychological religion? All my experiences had finally filled me with tremendous optimism and hope and exultation.

Did Nirvana really mean nonexistence? Or an expanded existence? Was it the same experience that the Christians called mystical union with God, Bucke called cosmic consciousness, Huxley and Sheldon and James termed mystical ecstasy, Jung called release of the deeper unconscious which led to the final "experience of God"? Was I plunging into the waters of abstraction over my head? I could see that this was the study of a lifetime. I had merely skimmed the surface. Or had I skimmed the cream itself?

The five steps in the awakening of man to the good in the self, in others, and in the universe were almost the same whether it was spontaneous and poetic or induced the Jungian psychology. Certainly the object of all the higher religions also was to arouse the noblest in man, make him love his neighbor as himself, and achieve final union with the ultimate good of the universe. And what steps did he go through to attain these three desirable ends?

Arnold Toynbee in *An Historian's Approach to Religion* informs us that there are today six higher living religions: Christianity, Islam, Hinduism, Judaism, Zoroastrianism, and Buddhism (Hinayana and Mahayana).

In all six of these disciplines he says the first three steps are fundamentally the same: an encounter first with suffering, then the "giving up self-centeredness"[5] (which feels like death), and "communication with the presence behind the phenomena"[6] (or rebirth which leads to love of others and desire to serve them and the cosmic principle). Some deeply religious persons do not feel the need of continuing through stages four and five — an understanding by Reason and final union of Reason with Intuition and Feeling to create the whole man.

In some religions however, intellectual instructions are offered first. As Swami Akhilananda says, Vedanta "first shows us how to understand intellectually the nature of God and then how to experience Him directly. In the process of understanding and experiencing God we develop love for our fellow beings."

Thus all religious awakenings are a psychological process which can be explained most scientifically by the Jungian theory of the laws governing the human psyche. And religious, psychological, or spontaneous and poetic awakening to the good traverse the same five steps.

But now suddenly there came upon me a terrible loneliness. Jung warns those who have achieved "self realization" or the release of the intuitive, ethical, esthetic collective unconscious that they will be lonely. I longed for congenial group life. But where to find it?

The religious did not believe in Freud or Jung or Sheldon.

The Freudian did not believe in the Jungians or art or religion. The Constitutionalists believed in the Developmentalists who followed Gesell but not in Freud. The Developmentalists did not believe in Freud or Jung, but in Sheldon. Artists knew little of Freud and less of Jung. Too many Christians condemned

Buddhism, Hinduism, and all other religions, and all psychologies, and were afraid of the sensuousness of the seven arts, ignoring their spiritual power.

So occasionally I turned on the radio on Sunday mornings. Out of curiosity I listened to ministers, rabbis, and priests. Invariably I turned it off absolutely sick at heart. Most of them were repeating the same old cliches I had heard as a child. Neither their words nor their voices were convincing. I did not believe they believed a word they said. I doubted if they understood a word they said. If they did, never in a million years would they make anyone else understand them. The pity of it! The utter, utter tragedy!

Today's bewildered frightened public longed for enlightenment. It was lying there in arm's reach in all its glorious shining abundance — neglected.

With all the temerity of a layman I concluded that what all religions all over the world needed was illumination by modern psychologies. How could they expect rational scientific man of today to believe even his own intuitive spiritual insight unless it was supported by the science of the human mind?

Why did all religions ignore all the painfully needed help that lay on the bookshop shelves — theirs for the reading? Why did not the religious leaders study Gesell's Developmental psychology and discover at what ages children **naturally** would be interested in religion? If the authorities believed in God why did they not study human nature — which He created? All psychologies were revelations of the natural God-given laws of the psyche.

In the case of adults, why did not the religious leaders study people according to Sheldon's Constitutional psychology? Then they could determine by physiques the type of temperament and thus teach others the natural way for them to evince religion.

Why did not man's spiritual guides — or their psychological associates — investigate to discover if a person was suffering from a neurosis which might be blocking his spiritual awakening? Then they might assist him in removing it.

Why not apply Jung's analytical therapy combined with their own spiritual methods to aid the person in achieving self-realization and a genuine religious experience?

Why could not people's deeper unconscious be aroused and stimulated to spiritual heights by great music, architecture, poetry, dancing, sculpture, and drama and painting? Intense study of Da Vinci's *Mona Lisa* was often better than a whole sermon.

Could not all the psychologies and all the arts bring all the higher religions new life and vitality? Could not this combination help the poor searching seeking frightened public cease to go through the motions of religion and begin to feel it deeply and live it daily? What would the human race gain if billions of people attended churches, temples, and synagogues if world wars continued between nations and hatred, cruelty, anguish, tension, and fear continued in individuals?

PART V

WHOLENESS

F.S.C. NORTHROP:
"The culture of the United States is initiating a shift to new philosophical foundations ... rooted in the intuitive ... aesthetic component [which] is immediately apprehensible and the theoretic component [which] is scientifically verifiable... The good society for the world must combine [them]."

CARL JUNG:
"The self is the total timeless man and corresponds to the mutual integration of conscious and unconscious."

CHAPTER 26

PHILOSOPHERS

RUSSELL

For years I had sought among the philosophers for the meaning of life, for guidance in conduct, for comfort in sorrow. They turned me away more confused than ever by the contradictions among themselves. There were more different systems than there were men. How could they all be correct? Why was there not one philosophy for all men? Truth was true, was it not? Or must we apply Sheldon again? Were our greatest thinkers conditioned even in their philosophy — by their own constitutional types?

Bertrand Russell himself answered that question in his *History of Philosophy*. "There is [a] way of classifying philosophies according to the predominant desire which . . . led the philosopher to philosophize. Thus we have philosophies of feeling; theoretical philosophies, inspired by a love of knowledge; and practical philosophies inspired by the love of action."[1]

In short, philosophy like religion, was viscerotonic, or cerebrotonic, or somatotonic. So philosophers thought according to their individual temperament and constitution, including the great and brilliant Russell himself, as he proved by his otherwise incredible remark, "The purpose of the mystic is to come as near as possible to nonexistence, which, for some reason never explained, he cannot achieve by suicide."[2] Obviously Russell himself for some reason he never explained, had not been fortunate enough to achieve a moment of intuitive insight into the nature of things, with a sense of union with the life force.[3]

Surely it was not nonexistence which the modern Western mystic sought but a larger fuller richer existence, here and now. Sometimes you felt as if you were absorbed into the infinite, sometimes you seemed to absorb it into yourself.

You lost your existence only to regain it enriched ten-fold.

Even Russell wrote, "Life must serve some end outside human life, an end which is impersonal and above mankind, such as God or truth or beauty. . .Contact with the eternal world — even if it be only a world of our imagining — brings strength and peace. . .To those who have known it once, it is the key of wisdom."[4]

I had enjoyed a delightful talk with Russell in New York years ago. He was amusing, kind, charming, and brilliant. His physique was slender and his long nose seemed to indicate an ectomorphic bone structure. Were the most brilliant intellectuals incapable of releasing the deeper layers of their unconscious? That was a problem I delegated to indefatigable investigators like Huxley or Jung or Sheldon.

EMERSON

There always had been something about Emerson that frightened me. I had admired him profoundly as a moral philosopher ever since I was twenty-five. Never should I forget the night he came to my rescue after the dull dinner party given me by the millionaire architect.

Yet invariably I shied away from the very word "Transcendentalism." I feared it was a kind of will-o-the-wisp which would lead me into a thick white emotional fog in which I should wander about and become lost forever. Now I must face the facts I had been avoiding all my life.

I consulted a fascinating and very illuminating little book by Charles Gelatt, "The Quaker Influence on Emerson" — a privately printed item. "Logically an intuitional or mystical epistomology denies any vital intellectual life."[5] But was it not possible to combine them? Was not that exactly what I was attempting to do now quite unsuccessfully?

"Emerson never could have denied the intellect, he was too much its product. What he wanted to find was inspiration; some phrase that would light his way to the proper mood for receiving mystical knowledge."[6] He seemed to have borrowed from the Quakers their belief in the "inner light." "Emerson moved away from the old, traditional view of God as a king on high. In many ways he seemed to follow the New Light theology. . . the conception of an Immanence rather than a God as the divine being."[7]

"We have vastly more kindness than is ever spoken, the whole human family is bathed with an element of love. . .If man lets the goodness from the Over-Soul flow through him, then is he all comprehending."[8] At last I was beginning to understand Emerson!

Certainly this confirmed my belief and experience that good and love were buried in all people. And by his term Over-Soul, did Emerson not mean the infinite good in the universe which seemed to flow through us whenever we were able to open the door of our deeper collective unconscious?

But why did Emerson deny personal immortality? Was it because, as Bucke said, he did not reach complete "cosmic consciousness"? (Certainly one glowing moment could convince any man even against his own reason.) Or were his experiences determined by his type of physique? Impossible to judge his type by old photographs.

I met the young man who chose to write on Emerson. His somatotype appeared to approximate 4-4-4. His temperament combined the warm friendliness of the viscerotonic with the ability to act (he was a highly successful businessman) of the somatotonic and the sensitivity and love of knowledge of the cerebrotonic. A brilliant intellectual who was also charming was an unusual combination.

OTHERS

Like a breeze I rushed through one book of philosophy after another listening only to the evidence which supported my case.

Plato said reason was the male principle of the universe, intuition the female principle. He believed in pre-existence. He also stated that man could discover truth in himself, by introspection, by remembering as I had remembered my twenty ecstasies.

He identified the essence of the universe with "the good."

Kant said in the realm of morals and religion, intuition and feeling must be exalted above reason and logic. Man seeks concord, nature gives him discord to make him grow. Did this explain evil?

All my great spiritual renascence had been precipitated by the most ghastly struggle. We human beings simply did not understand the fundamental laws of the human psyche.

Kant further said that the human capacity for knowledge was limited. Our minds were unable to comprehend the intrinsic nature of "things-in-themselves." But certain things, like the existence of a God and immortality could be believed because in some realms instinct and feeling are more trustworthy than reason.

Bergson said ultimately reality was not an inaccessible absolute but could be apprehended by man. "In the absolute we live and move and have our being." Our intellect sees reality as a dead mechanism but intuition reveals spiritual life.

Even **Aristotle** said everything on earth is moved by an inner urge to grow into something greater than it is and the goal of the world's growth is that magnetic power — God.

To have many of my views for which I had struggled alone, doubtful and afraid now corroborated by some of the greatest of the philosophers filled me with a deep serene gratification.

NORTHROP

Then the greatest plum of all fell right into my lap. A book which many scholarly critics had hailed as one of the great books of this century, *The Meeting of East and West* by F.S.C. Northrop. I met and talked with him briefly after his return to Yale from India. He was of the constitutional type which "had everything" — fine physique and face, warmth, humor, charm, vast erudition and he was capable of tremendous activity — probably a 4-4-4 in physique.

Northrop, the scholar, approached modern problems on the international and philosophical level. Was not I, as a layman, attempting to approach them on the individual and psychological level? He believed there never would be permanent peace until Western man — scientific, rational, political, and materialistic — learned to understand the intuitive aesthetic (perceived by feeling) insights of the East — and vice versa.[9] In psychological terms, was that not equivalent to releasing the best in our subconscious minds and reuniting it with our conscious reason? Would nations, however, not be obliged to follow individuals?

"There will be no culture," Northrop stated, "which adequately meets the spiritual as well as the intellectual needs of men until...the female aesthetic intuitive principle in things speaks in its purity"...[10]

"This immediately apprehended component of things...must be taken as primary and ultimate. Here seems to be something self-evident and basic upon which an America and a world fighting their way from faiths that have failed them can build[11]...The undifferentiated, passionately moving, ineffable aesthetic continuum[12]...[is] what is meant by tao, jen. Nirvana, and Brahman[13]...The psychic character of the self is identical with the cosmic principle of the universe[14]...The undifferentiated aesthetic continuum [is] common to all persons[15]...

"The culture of the United States is initiating a shift to a new philosophical foundation...rooted in the intuitive...aesthetic component [which] is immediately apprehensible and the theoretic component [which] is scientifically verifiable."[16]

Northrop seemed to believe that the Orient must learn how to amass material wealth like that produced by our science and reason in order to abolish their poverty and disease. The Occident must revive in itself the intuitive aesthetic apprehension known to the East, in order to nourish the inner spiritual man. Reason and Intuition must reunite to make the whole man.

As I read, I was obliged to close Northrop's book time and time again. I feared the wave of intellectual excitement would sweep me out of the room. I must wait till it subsided so my poor brain might function again. Finally I closed the book, gripping the volume in both hands with such intense feeling I all but broke its hard covers.

Overwhelmed — waiting — waiting — while a warm golden liquid light seemed to expand, radiate, through my blood and flesh, my mind and spirit, and all my senses.

Now it was so vivid, so real, it was a physical sensation. Suddenly I could feel my conscious mind opening wide and warm to accept the deepest thrusts of my unconscious. In a burst of incredible glory they were made one! Then I felt fulfilled, complete, serene, and warmly exultant.

Now, I knew, and I knew that I knew — my reason and logic had united with my intuition and feeling.

And I was made whole from that hour!

But a psychologist set the final crown on my search by Reason for a rational explanation of my own twenty ecstatic awakenings to the good in the self, in others, and in the universe.

My husband and I returned from Europe and the first thing I did was to purchase Sheldon's latest book, *Atlas of Men*. Of course there was a slight difference in the somatotypes of men and women. I turned first to my own somatotype, the 4-4-4. Had Sheldon made any new discoveries about it? What I read staggered me:

"At the top, at the peak and center, sits the 4-4-4. He alone looks down all three major slopes. Viewed from any position except his own, perhaps, the psychological position of the 4-4-4 looks more like a predicament than a position. . .The 4-4-4 occasionally seems to succeed in combining the warm and social binding-together quality of viscerotonia with both the driving power of somatotonia and the time-binding quality of far-sightedness of cerebrotonia. The 4-4-4 is then a superb, and perhaps an **elevated** personality — man's nearest approach to his persistent vision of Divinity, who he maintains is motivationally a 7-7-7, at once all-loving, omnipotent and omniscient."[17]

So whether spontaneous or induced, the release of man's ethical, intuitive, loving, spiritual self from its concealment in the collective unconscious was constitutional, perhaps evolutional, undoubtedly physiological, also religious, poetic, and sometimes philosophical, and positively psychological!!!

CODA:

ESSAY ON THE WHOLE MAN

AWAKENING

So I say to myself
And I say to you
If you are in despair
About the political chaos of the world
And the moral decline of modern man
If all the reason you possess
And all the education you've received
Fail to solve the world's most urgent problems
Of hate and hostility
Between men and nations
If you are in despair about yourself
A misfit in a contemporary society
That worships nothing — or little —
Save science and reason
Politics and materialism
Which in spite of untold benefits
Leave the inner man
With untold emptiness
And the outer world
With daily-told disasters
If the overt behavior of men
With their wars and bombs
Their cruelty, dishonor, and deception

Seem to prove man innately evil
And so destroys your faith
In the human race;
If you discover to your horror
That without this faith
Life is scarcely worth the living —
Despite your private happiness —
If you finally drown in your own despair
Concerning the world
And you cry aloud
What shall I do to be saved?
And no one comes to your rescue —
And no one will —
If you seem to die —
For what is despair but a living death? —
You can be saved
Even born again
For nature moves in mysterious ways
Her wonders to perform.

THE SEARCH WITHIN

But nature helps those
Who help themselves
So search for the good in man
Look for what he intrinsically IS
Not what he has DONE
To destroy the peace of the world
By his own misguided actions:
Has he no infallible inner guide?
No perennial clarity of vision?
No indestructible hierarchy of values?
On the answer to this urgent question
Depends our very lives and sanity
And the future of the entire world
For we never will have a better world
Until we have better people in it
Tragic events have proved **that** recently —
But you cannot change human nature —
True —
But we can find ways to awaken the dormant good,
The latent love,
Inherent in all men.
We must, if we are to survive;

We must look inward
As well as outward
Make peace with ourselves
Before we can make peace with others
Learn to love ourselves
Before we can love others
Remember Alexander Pope
And his famous Essay of Man?
"Reason, passion, answer one great aim
That true self love and social are the same
And all our knowledge, ourselves to know."[1]
So again I say
Search for the good in man
Where? but in yourself
Search for the God-in-man
Where? but in yourself.

SELF-REALIZATION

But I say to myself
And I say to you of the Western world
However successful other methods
For other older races,
Follow the deepest laws
Of your own Western nature
Conditioned for centuries by science and reason
Mesomorphic action and physique
Seek the release of your better self
Through fulfillment not renunciation
Through acceptance of life not rejection
Through love and passion not asceticism
By immersing yourself in nature
Not retreating from it
By submitting to the natural rhythms of the body
Not by mortifying it
By service to your fellowman
Not selfish solitude — except periodically;
Seek the good life
Through contemplation
And also the absence of it
Through harmony with the laws of nature
Not their reversal
Through active participation in life
Not withdrawal — except periodically.

WHAT'S IN A NAME?

So call it what you will,
This warm golden expansiveness
By any name would be as sweet
Call it ecstasy as the poets do
Or intuitive insight
Into the nature of things
With a sense of union with the life force
As some philosophers prefer,
Or direct aesthetic intuitive apprehension
Of "the undifferentiated aesthetic continuum"[2]
As Northrop does
Or call it the higher mystical thought
Our pure reason prepares us for
Leading to "reverence for life"
As Albert Schweitzer terms it.
Or think of it
As an experience of God
As Christians do in the West
Or like the Buddhists
Define it as Enlightenment and Nirvana
Or speak of it as Illumination
As the Hindus do.
Or with the followers of Lao-Tzu
See it as mystical harmony with Tao,
By any name it is rewarding.

Or call it by various names
Of the various psychologists
Professional or literary
Call it mysticism
With James and Sheldon
Huxley and Woolf
Or "cosmic consciousness"
To use Bucke's term —
If you qualify it —
Or the release of our collective unconscious
Leading to self-realization and individuation
As Jung expresses it.

Whatever the terminology
Poetic or philosophic
Religious or psychological
Whatever the superstructure added afterward

The basic experience is the same — **psychologically**
An upwelling of our deeper unconscious
Where the spiritual impulse is buried
Leading to a sense of union
With the cosmic order of things.

THE ABSOLUTE

Someday science may split the last atom
Of man's ignorance
Break the sound barrier
Which guards the infinite
Till then, flashes of poetic intuition
Precede slow science by hundreds of years
Even Einstein says the mystical experience
Is the precursor of all true science.
If there is no cosmic principle
Why does the intuitive perception
And the ecstatic emotion
Of so many great men
In so many countries
Throughout written history
Inform them that there is?
Does nature deal in falsehoods?

But the modern intellectual
Demands scientific explanation
Even of his spiritual experiences
So if the psychologists
Can satisfy the scientists
That the religious urge is inherent
In the deepest layers of man's unconscious,
As primary as hunger and sex
And equally dangerous to ignore,
The battle of the centuries may be won,
Science and religion may meet at long last
And John Dewey's prophecy come true;
The religious spirit will be revivified
Because it will be in harmony
With man's scientific beliefs.
If Aristotle and Aquinas say
The unknown is knowable through Reason
And Northrop and Jung say
It is knowable through intuition
Or the collective unconscious

Then surely the spirit of the universe
Can be apprehended
Both by reason
And intuition
So why all the argument?

VINDICATION

So I ask myself
And I ask modern man
Can we vindicate the ways of man to God?
Has our sacred science,
Infallible reason,
Golden materialism,
And perfect political systems,
Tossed into the dust heap
The jewel without price?
The primary source of ultimate human happiness
And our last chance
For permanent world peace?
Has modern man sold his birthright?
And for what?
The atom bomb?
Perpetual war?
And permanent despair?

Time is running out
Radioactivity is running in
Soon it will be too late
Yet if man can reestablish
His relation to the universe
Through his own subconscious mind —
By whatever means
His best defense against atomic destruction
May be a psychological weapon
Or spiritual
For they are the same.

To modern man in general
And the intellectual in particular
Maturity may bring
A second flowering
Thoughtful despair deeply felt
May bring to our rescue
A blossoming of the intuitive seeds

Buried too long in the dark
Of the deeper unconscious
And reason, like a strong straight stem
Will support these delicate mystical flowers
Thus vindicating the ways of man to God
Thus producing a rational mysticism,
And perhaps a spiritual psychology
Or a psychological religion
For a better tomorrow.

CERTITUDE

So when we pursue universal truths
We may "lose our life to find it"
"Die," and be born again
But our steep ascent
Up the mighty marble steps
Of Despair, Death, and Rebirth,
Reason, and Wholeness,
Finally leads us
To the high place called certitude.
Bertrand Russell says
Of the man beyond logic
Who has had mystical experiences —
He has been there. He **knows.**[3]
Well, I have been there,
I know. I know
There are rare moments of exaltation
Aroused spontaneously
By sea or sun or wind
By the ennobling power of great music
The purifying principle in fine painting
By thinking a thought
Dancing a dance
Even kissing a kiss;
Enlightening moments
When we receive flashes
Of intuitive insight
Into the nature of things
Luminous moments
When we unite — or seem to —
With the infinite unknown.
I know our mystical moments,
Or liberation of the subconscious,

Will reveal the meaning of life
The nature of the self
The universe
And man's relation to it
Even the nature of the ideal society,
And if reason rejects
Our intuitive insights
And it will
And it should
We may not find — yet —
Sufficient scientific verification
But we can find rational explanations.

So whether our awakening
Is spontaneous — as mine was —
Or deliberately induced
By a philosophy like Northrop's
Or a psychology like Jung's
Or any of the higher religions
Revivified by the modern psychologies,
Our victorious quest
For the good in ourselves
And therefore the good in others
And therefore the good in the universe
Brings us immeasurable rewards.

REWARDS

The triumphant search
For ultimate reality
Brings us
Peace of mind
A sense of security
Greater rapport with nature
Deeper response to the arts
A love of our fellow men
Of which we did not believe ourselves capable
New concepts of the ideal society.
It awakens spontaneous love
Of our neighbors as ourselves,
Makes humanitarians of us all
Awakens the dormant good
Inherent in all men
Brings the philosophical certitude
We had sought all our lives.

It brings a sense of wholeness
Reunion of our reason and intuition
A wedding of logic and feeling
Or acceptance by our conscious mind
Of our deeper unconscious
Where the gods of the race abide.
And finally
Our victorious search for ultimate answers
Unites us with the cosmic principal
Brings the death of fear
An end to the fear of death
With Walt Whitman we learn
To "laugh at what you call dissolution."[4]
For it brings us intimations
Of immortality
Acceptable to reason heretofore intractable
It revives our dying faith
In ourselves, in mankind
And in the supreme good of the universe.

THE INEVITABLE SEARCH

And so ends the search
The inevitable search
That comes when the world's moral maladies
Are at their worst —
As they are today —
When the individual's despair
Is at its deepest —
As it is today —
The search for what the philosophers call
Ultimate Reality
And the religious call
God
And the Jungian psychologists term
Self-realization and individuation
Leading to a spiritual experience.

Perhaps the man of tomorrow
Will demand a synthesis
Comprehensive enough to embrace
Philosophy and religion,
Psychology and aesthetics
For if we draw the lines long enough
From these four disciplines

Ultimately they meet in space,
At the point of the eternal mystery
Producing — perhaps in a foreseeable future
A cosmic psychology
Or a psychological religion
Which may — at some not too distant day —
Bring to perennially warring nations
Permanent peace
And prosperity for all
Love of man for his fellows,
An awakening to Ultimate Reality
And communication with the eternal presence
Behind the world's phenomena.

— End —

APPENDIX

Grateful acknowledgment is made to all those authors and publishers who granted me permission to make direct quotations from their books — listed below — on which they hold copyrights.

Numbers in parenthesis correspond to superior numbers throughout the text referring in most cases to direct quotations, but occasionally to unquoted passages.

Bibliography contains other important books consulted.

PART I — DESPAIR

Bucke, Richard Maurice. *Cosmic Consciousness*. New York: E. P. Dutton and Co., Inc., 1948.

Dante Alighieri. *The Divine Comedy*. New York: P.F. Collier & Son, 1909.

Emerson, Ralph Waldo. *Essays, First Series*. Boston: Houghton, Mifflin and Co., 1903

Freud, Sigmund. *Basic Writings: Psychopathology of Everyday Life, Interpretation of Dreams, Three Contributions to the Theory of Sex, Wit and Its Relation to the Unconscious, Totem and Taboo, History of the Psychoanalytic Movement*. New York: Modern Library, Random House, 1938. *General Introduction to Psychoanalysis*. New York: Liveright Publishing Corp., 1935. *New Introductory Lectures on Psychoanalysis*. New York: W. W. Norton & Co., Inc., 1933. *An Outline of Psychoanalysis*. New York: W. W. Norton & Co., Inc., 1949.

Harding, M. Esther. *Journey Into Self*. New York: Longmans, Green and Co., 1956.

Huxley, Aldous. *Doors of Perception*. New York: Harper & Brothers, 1954.

James, William. *Varieties of Religious Experience*. New York: Longmans, Green and Co., Inc., 1902, p. 108. (14)

John. *Bible*. 3:3 (8)

Jung, Carl G. *Two Essays on Analytical Psychology*. New York: Bollingen Series XX, Pantheon Books, 1953, p. 171. (3) *Practice of Psychotherapy*. New York: Bollingen Series XX, Pantheon Books, 1954, p. 290. (4) *Modern Man in Search of a Soul*. New York: Harcourt, Brace and Co., 1933, p. 275. (5) *Psychology and Religion*. New Haven: Yale University Press, 1938, p. 73 (6) *Integration of the Personality*. London: Routledge & Keegan Paul Ltd., 1950. *Essays on Contemporary Events*. London: Keegan Paul, 1947.

Jung (books on) Glover, Edward. *Freud or Jung*. New York: W. W. Norton & Co., Inc., 1950.
Harding, M. Esther. *Psychic Energy*. New York: Bollingen Series XX, Pantheon Books, 1948.

Jacobi, Jolan. *Psychology of Jung*. New Haven: Yale University Press, 1943.

Progoff, Ira. *Jung's Psychology and Its Social Meaning*. New York: Julian Press, Inc., 1953. *Death and Rebirth of Psychology*. New York: Julian Press, Inc., 1956.

Kant, Immanuel. *Natural Principle of the Political Order Considered in Connection with the Idea of a Universal Cosmopolitical History*.

Matthew. *Bible*. 10:39. (7), (15)

Millay, Edna. *Renascence*. New York: Harper & Brothers, 1917, p. 6 (10), p. 8 (11), p. 10 (12), p. 12 (13)

Northrop, F. S. C. *Meeting of East and West*. New York: Macmillan Co., 1946.

Plato. *The Republic*.

Progoff, Ira. *Death and Rebirth of Psychology*. New York: Julian Press, 1956, pages 3, 4, 44, 255, (9)

Sheldon, William. *Varieties of Human Physique*. New York: Harper and Brothers, 1940. *Varieties of Temperament*. New York: Harper and Brothers, 1944. *Psychology and the Promethean Will*. New York: Harper and Brothers, 1936. *Atlas of Men*. New York: Harper and Brothers, 1954.

Toynbee, Arnold. *An Historian's Approach to Religion*. New York: Oxford University Press, 1956, p. 275 (1), p. 288 (2)

Whitman, Walt. *Leaves of Grass*. New York: Doubleday, Doran & Co., MCMXL.

Wordsworth, William W. *Complete Poetical Works*. New York: Thomas Y. Crowell. (Ode, Intimations of Immortality From Recollections of Early Childhood.)

PART II — "DEATH"

Coleridge, Samuel Taylor. *Kubla Kahn*. New York: P. F. Collier & Son, 1910. The Harvard Classics, Vol. 41, p. 719, (5)

Emerson, Ralph Waldo. *Essays, First Series*. (Over-Soul). Boston: Houghton, Mifflin and Co., 1903, p. 282 (3)

James, William. *Varieties of Religious Experience*. New York: Longmans, Green & Co., Inc., 1902, p. 108, (4)

Jung, Carl G. *Practice of Psychotherapy*. New York: Bollingen Series XX, Pantheon Books, 1954, p. 290 (6)

Millay, Edna. *Renascence*. New York: Harper & Brothers, 1917, p. 6 (1)

Wordsworth, William. *Wordsworth's Poems (Ode — Intimations of Immortality from Recollections of Early Childhood)*. New York: Thomas Y. Crowel Co., p. 404 (2)

PART III — REBIRTH
CHAPTER 6 — FLOWERS

Shelley, Percy Bysshe. *Complete Poetical Works*. London: Oxford University Press, 1917, p. 574 (1)

CHAPTER 7 — CHILDREN

Wordsworth, William. *Complete Poetical Works of —*. New York: Thomas Crowell & Co., (Ode, Intimation of Immortality From Recollections of Early Childhood.) Author's Introduction, p. 403 (1), Ode, p. 403 (2), p. 404 (3), Author's Introduction, p. 403 (4)

CHAPTER 8 — POETRY

James, William. *Varieties of Religious Experience*. New York: Longmans, Green & Co., Inc., 1902, p. 109 (4)

Swinburne, Algernon Charles. *Poems*. New York: Modern Library, (Hertha), p. 170 (1), (2), p. 171 (3)

CHAPTER 9 — THOUGHT

Emerson, Ralph Waldo. *Essays, First Series.* Boston: Houghton, Mifflin & Co., 1903, Intellect, p. 329 (2), p. 330 (4); Self-Reliances, p. 45 (3), p. 74 (5), p. 45 (6); Over-Soul, p. 270 (7), p. 280 (8)
Kings II. *Bible.* 2:11 (1)

CHAPTER 12 — SEA AND SAND

Buddha, *Teachings of the Compassionate* —. New York: New American Library, 1955, p. 161 (1)
Huxley, Aldous. *Do What You Will.* New York: Harper and Brothers, 1929, (Spinoza's Worm . Pascal.) *Texts and Pretexts.* New York: Harper and Brothers, 1932. *Ends and Means.* New York: Harpers and Brothers, 1937, p. 272 (3)
Underhill, Evelyn. *Mysticism.* London: Methuen & Co., Ltd. (Sufi authors) (2), p. 462 (4)

CHAPTER 15 — PAINTING

Aristotle. *Poetics.*

CHAPTER 16 — MUSIC

Charpentier. *Louise.* (Libretto.) New York: Steinway & Sons.

CHAPTER 18 — SCULPTURE

Rodin, Auguste. *Art.* Boston: Small, Maynard & Co., 1912, p. 178 (1), p. 165 (2), 177 (3), 183 (4)

CHAPTER 19 — ARCHITECTURE

Adams, Henry. *Mont Saint Michel and Chartres.* Boston: Houghton, Mifflin Co., 1905, p. 34 (1)
Rand, Ayn. *The Fountainhead.* Indianapolis: Bobbs-Merrill Co., 1943

CHAPTER 22 — SUMMER

Jefferson, Thomas.
Rand, Ayn. *The Fountainhead.* Indianapolis: Bobbs-Merrill Co., 1943, 173 (1)
Whitman, Walt. *Leaves of Grass.* New York: Doubleday, Doran & Co., Inc., MCMXL, p. 34 (1), 179 (2), 300 (3) (in Preface to 1855 edition).

PART IV — REASON
CHAPTER 23 — PSYCHOLOGISTS

Bucke, Richard Maurice. *Cosmic Consciousness.* New York: E. P. Dutton and Co., Inc., 1948, p. 51 (23), p. 79 (24)
Freud, Sigmund. *New Introductory Lectures on Psychoanalysis.* New York: W. W. Norton & Co., Inc., 1933. *Basic Writings of Sigmund Freud: Psychopathology of Everyday Life, Interpretation of Dreams, Three Contributions to the Theory of Sex, Wit and Its Relation to the Unconscious, Totem and Taboo, History of the Psychoanalytic Movement.* New York: Modern Library, 1938. *An Outline of Psychoanalysis.* New York: W. W. Norton & Co., Inc., 1949. *A General Introduction to Psychoanalysis.* New York: Liveright Publishing Corp., 1935.
Gesell, Arnold and Frances Ilg. *Infant and Child in the Culture of Today.* New York: Harper & Brothers, 1943. *The Child From Five to Ten.* New York: Harper and Brothers,

1946 (In collaboration with Louise Bates Ames and Glenna Bullis).
Glover, Edward. *Freud or Jung*. New York: W. W. Norton & Co., Inc., 1950.
Harding, M. Esther. *Psychic Energy*. New York: Bollingen Series X, Pantheon Books, 1948, p. 151 (38)
Huxley, Aldous. *Do What You Will*. New York: Harper & Brothers, p. 268 (8), p. 67 (9). *Doors of Perception*. New York: Harper and Brothers, 1954, p. 18 (10), title (11), *Ends and Means*. New York: Harper & Brothers, 1937, p. 306 (12). *Olive Tree*. New York: Harper & Brothers, 1937, p. 208 (40). *Texts and Pretexts*. New York: Harper & Brothers, 1932. *Themes and Variations*. New York: Harper & Brothers, 1950. *Perennial Philosophy*. New York: Harper & Brothers, 1945.
Jacobi, Jolan. *Psychology of Jung*. New Haven: Yale University Press, 1943, p. 140 (29)
James, Williams. *Varieties of Religious Experience*. New York: Longmans, Green & Co., Inc., 1902 (?), p. 401 (13), p. 58 (14), p. 478 (15), (16), p. 162 (17), p. 163 (18), p. 475 (19), (20), p. 53 (21), p. 370 (22), p. 503 (39).
Jung, Carl G. *Practice of Psychotherapy*. New York: Bollingen Series XX, Pantheon Books, 1954, p. 290 (25), p. 12 (26), p. 153 (27). *Modern Man's Search for a Soul*. New York: Harcourt, Brace & Co., 1933, p. 275 (28), p. 55 (37). *Two Essays on Analytical Psychology*. New York: Bollingen Series XX, Pantheon Books, 1953, p. 70 (30), p. 26 (32). *Psychology and Religion*, New Haven: Yale University Press, 1938, p. 73 (31), p. 104 (33), p. 95 (34), p. 104-5 (35), p. 113 (36).
Progoff, Ira. *Death and Rebirth of Psychology*. New York: Julian Press, 1956. *Jung's Psychology and Its Social Meaning*. New York: Julian Press, 1953.
Sheldon, William H. *Varieties of Temperament*. New York: Harper and Brothers, 1944, p. 275 (1), (2), p. 276 (3). *Psychology and the Promethean Will*. New York: Harper and Brothers, 1936, p. 229 (4), p. 104-5 (5), p. 123 (6), p. 223 (7). *Varieties of Human Physique*. New York: Harper and Brothers, 1940.

CHAPTER 24 — POETS

Bucke, Richard Maurice. *Cosmic Consciousness*. New York: E. P. Dutton and Co., Inc., 1948, p. 227 (1)
Dante Alighieri. *The Divine Comedy*. New York: Harvard Classic, Collier & Son, 1909, Canto XXX, p. 413 (11), 413 (12), 414 (13), 415 (14)
Millay, Edna. *Renascence*. New York: Harper and Brothers, 1917, p. 6 (5), 12 (6), 4 (7), 4-5 (8)
Whitman, Walt. *Leaves of Grass*. New York: Doubleday, Doran & Co., Inc., MCMXL, p. 298 (2) (Preface to the 1855 edition), p. 218 (4). *Leaves of Grass*. New York: Modern Library, 1922, p. 195 (3)
Wordsworth, William. *Complete Poetical Works*. New York: Thomas Y. Crowell, (?), p. 403 (10), 404 (9)

PART IV — REASON
CHAPTER 25 — BIBLES

Akhilananda. *Hindu Psychology*. New York: Harper & Brothers, 1946.
Author Unknown. *Bhagavad-Gita*. New York: New American Library, 1955.
Buddha. *Teachings of the Compassionate Buddha*. Edited by E. A. Burtt. New York: New American Library, 1955.
Confucius. *Sayings of Confucius* (Analects). New York: New American Library, 1957. (Translated by James R. Ware.)
Huxley, Aldous. *Perennial Philosophy*. New York: Harper and Brothers, 1945.
John. *Bible*. 3:3 (3)
Lao Tzu. *Way of Life*. New York: New American Library, 1955.

Levy, John. *The Nature of Man According to the Vedanta.* London: Routledge & Keegan Paul, 1956.
Life Magazine editors. *World's Great Religions.* New York: Time, Inc., 1957.
Luke. *Bible.* 17:21. (1)
Matthew. *Bible.* 18:3 (2), 16:25 (4)
Mohammed. *Koran.*
Northrop, F. S. C. *Meeting of East and West.* New York: Macmillan Co., 1946.
Suzuki, D. T. *Zen Buddhism.* Garden City, N.Y. Doubleday & Co., 1956.
Toynbee, Arnold. *An Historian's Approach to Religion.* New York: Oxford University Press, 1956, p. 275 (5), p. 288 (6)
Underhill, Evelyn. *Mysticism.* London: Methuen & Co., Ltd., 1952. *The Mystic Way.* London, J. M. Dent & Co., 1913
Unknown Author. *Upanishads.* New York: New American Library, 1957.
Yogananda, Paramhansa. *Autobiography of a Yogi.* Los Angeles: Self-Realization Fellowship, 1956.

PART V — WHOLENESS
CHAPTER 26 — PHILOSOPHERS

Anshen, Ruth Nanda. Editor. *Science of Culture Series.* New York: Vol. I-III Harcourt, Brace & Co., 1940. New York: Vol. IV-VI Harper & Brothers, 1947. Editor, *World Perspective Series.* New York: Harper & Brothers, 1954.
Aristotle. *Metaphysics.*
Bergson, Henri. *Creative Evolution.*
Emerson, Ralph Waldo. *Journals, Vol. IV.* Boston, 1909, p. 305 (8). *Essays, First Series.* Boston: Houghton Mifflin Co., 1905.
Gelatt, Charles D. *Quaker Influence on Emerson.* Privately Printed. p. 55 (4), 76 (5), 76 (6), 102 (7)
Kant, Immanuel. *Critique of Practical Reason.*
Northrop, F. S. C. *Meeting of East and West.* New York: Macmillan Co., 1946, p. 478 (9), 463 (10), 162 (11), 367 (12), 372 (13), 463 (14), 337 (15), 163 (16)
Plato. *Phaedrus. Symposium. Republic.*
Russell, Bertrand. *History of Western Philosophy.* New York: Simon and Schuster, 1945, p. 792 (1), 757 (2). *Selected Papers: (Mysticism and Logic,* p. 29 (3); *Why Men Fight; Proposed Roads to Freedom; Education and the Good Life).* London: Allen & Unwin, 1927.
Sheldon, William H. *Atlas of Men.* New York: Harper and Brothers, 1954, p. 222 (17)
Sinnott, Edmund Ware. *Biology of the Spirit.* New York: Viking Press, 1955. *Matter, Mind and Man.* New York: Harper & Brothers, 1957.

ESSAY ON THE WHOLE MAN

Northorp, F. S. C. *Meeting of East and West.* New York: Macmillan Co., 1946, p. 370 (2)
Pope, Alexander. *English Poetry. Harvard Classics.* New York: P. F. Collier & Son, 1910 (An Essay on Man), p. 451 (1)
Russell, Bertrand. *Mysticism and Logic.* London: Allen & Unwin, 1951. (3)
Schweitzer, Albert. *The World of —* (Anderson and Exman) New York: Harper & Brothers, 1955.
Whitman, Walt. *Leaves of Grass. (Song of Myself —* part 20). New York: Doubleday, Doran & Co., MCMXL, p. 56 (4)

INDEX

www.ingramcontent.com/pod-product-compliance
Lightning Source LLC
Chambersburg PA
CBHW072143270326
41931CB00010B/1869